Do you get ner ✔ **KU-735-341**
What are the best ways of constructing a speech?
Why do some jokes fall flat — and how can you
make sure they don't? What are the most dangerous
aspects of a press or TV interview, and how can
you guard against them? How can debating skills
help you in everyday disputes?

This book teaches you the full range of public
speaking skills — for use in your job, on social
occasions, at conferences, with the news media and
in formal debating. You will learn how to present
yourself well, how to use humour effectively, how
to research and build your speech, and more compelling ways of using language and imagery.

Dick Smithies is highly skilled in all forms of public
speaking, as champion debater, top adjudicator,
teacher of speaking skills, and guest at conferences
and social events. Into this book he packs all the
knowledge he has gained over the years from both
speaking and from tutoring other speakers.

The HOW TO Series

HOW TO COPE WITH CREDIT AND DEAL WITH DEBT
Ann Andrews and Peter Houghton

HOW TO FACE THE INTERVIEW
And Other Selection Procedures
Clive Fletcher

HOW TO FORM A LIMITED COMPANY FOR £50
Complete With All The Forms You Need
Barry Sheppard

HOW NOT TO GET RIPPED OFF
Barbara Lantin

HOW TO PASS EXAMS
And How To Prepare For Them With Less Anxiety
Fred Orr

HOW TO SPEAK IN PUBLIC
A Winning Way With Words
Dick Smithies

HOW TO SPLIT UP – AND SURVIVE FINANCIALLY
Tony Hetherington

HOW TO SUCCEED AT WORK
Fred Orr

HOW TO

SPEAK IN PUBLIC

A WINNING WAY WITH WORDS

DICK SMITHIES

UNWIN PAPERBACKS

London   Sydney

First published in Australia and New Zealand by Unwin Paperbacks in association with the Port Nicholson Press in 1985

First published in Great Britain by Unwin Paperbacks in 1987

UNWIN HYMAN LIMITED
Denmark House
37–39 Queen Elizabeth Street
LONDON SE1 2QB
and
40 Museum Street, LONDON WC1A 1LU

Allen & Unwin Australia Pty Ltd
8 Napier Street, North Sydney, NSW 2060, Australia

Unwin Paperbacks with Port Nicholson Press
60 Cambridge Terrace, Wellington, New Zealand

British Library Cataloguing in Publication Data

Smithies, Dick
  How to speak in public : a winning way
  with words. ——— (The How to series)
  1. Public speaking
  I. Title
  808.5'1   PN4121
  ISBN 0–04–370202–3

Printed and bound in Great Britain
by Cox & Wyman Ltd, Reading

CONTENTS

THE FUTURE BELONGS TO
THOSE WHO COMMUNICATE WELL

Yes, of course you can become a competent public speaker. Of course you can control those nervous flutterings in your stomach. Of course you can handle social speeches with aplomb. Of course you can present yourself well at a job interview. Of course you can analyse and interpret contentious issues – and you can argue as persuasively and coherently as anyone.

I know you can achieve these goals because I have helped hundreds of others to do so. For fifteen years at the Imps public speaking club I have watched tongue-tied and self-conscious novices gain confidence, growing visibly in the fluency and insight of their arguments. Good speakers are not born: they are made.

In this book you will learn how to overcome fear of standing before a strange audience. You will learn how to prepare beforehand – how to research and plan, how to get ideas and how to use them, and how to structure your message. There's a chapter on what to do when your audience dislikes you in advance: you will see how not to get offside with your listeners, how to persuade people to your point of view, how to handle that difficult question and answer period. In another chapter you will discover that good use of humour is not restricted to a favoured few: anyone can make people laugh. Two more chapters deal with improving your skills – the skills of writing and speaking, and the skills of presentation that experienced speakers use. Part Two covers speeches for different situations: social speeches, job interviews and discussions at work, chairing a meeting, and media interviews. Finally, there is a section on the skills of debate, which are useful to all forms of public speaking.

The ability to speak well, to large or small gatherings, or to one other person, is essential to everyday life. You must stick up for yourself in a world where articulate people often use verbal skills without scruple, trampling upon the opinions of the timid and diffident. With vehemence, eloquence and sheer force of personality, they dominate others. Learning the simple techniques of public speaking will enable your point of view to be heard, and your position to be respected.

What I have to say here applies equally to men and women. Some books on public speaking suggest that women have more difficulty with these skills than men: this is simply not true. Some women have light voices; so too do some men. Some men can summon stentorian volume of voice; so too can some women. A person with a light voice, whether male or female, has to be helped to overcome that difficulty in public speaking. All the techniques I describe here are as available to women as they are to men.

A foreign accent is sometimes thought of as a handicap in public speaking. Quite the reverse. An accent always adds interest, causes people to listen more intently, and provides pleasing variety to the ear. Even speech impediments need not be a bar. I have never known a person so handicapped that he or she could not be turned into a competent speaker.

Go to it. Use this book and take from it what you will. Decide for yourself what is good in human communication. Experiment. Practise. Remember that no-one is on form on every occasion: so don't be despondent if once in a while things go wrong. Bounce back.

In much of the world freedom of speech is under threat; elsewhere it has largely disappeared. It is upon this most basic of our liberties that democracy is founded – the cut and counter-thrust of debate and discussion. Don't hold back. Enter the fray. Start developing a winning way with words.

Part One

BUILDING YOUR SPEAKING SKILLS

Chapter One

HOW TO CONQUER YOUR NERVOUSNESS ABOUT SPEAKING IN PUBLIC

Nearly everyone is nervous at the thought of speaking in public. Such anxiety is normal and natural. It should be confessed without shame. For stage fright can be overcome. No matter how great your fears, you can learn simple techniques that will give you confidence.

In the course of this chapter you will learn what happens to your body when you are seized by fear of confronting an audience. You will learn how to ease your bodily tensions. You will discover how to quiet your anxieties. Above all, you will learn two infallible ways of controlling platform nervousness, even after it has begun gripping you.

I am not going to give you vague theories. Drawing upon my fifteen years of teaching public speaking, I will list for you the techniques I have seen succeed again and again. There are tricks of the trade you can use just one hour after reading this chapter which will greatly reduce your fear of confronting an audience.

The first thing to understand is that you are not alone. A few years ago some American researchers asked 3,000 people what it was they feared most. The possibilities were endless: blindness, bereavement, painful illness, disfigurement, unemployment, and so on. But amazingly the single largest group, 40 per cent, gave speaking before a large audience as the affliction they most dreaded.

Take comfort from this. Most people share your nervousness. It is perfectly natural that people who are skilful and accomplished in other activities become incapacitated when asked to do no more than speak in public. Throughout history great men – Napoleon, Disraeli, George Bernard Shaw, Winston Churchill, Abraham Lincoln – have confessed that fear marred their early speaking performances.

No experienced speaker or politician or comedian or actor or television personality wants to eliminate nervousness entirely. A little bit of platform nerves is a great asset. It keys you up and ensures you will give of your best. Any speaker who is entirely relaxed runs the risk of being flat and dull.

So if you never wholly conquer your nervousness, this is a plus. You will be on a par with all those urbane TV interviewers, stage actors and political pundits who, despite years of experience, still become keyed up just before a big speaking occasion.

And not just speakers. Footballers are commonly full of trepidation before a big game, tennis players before the final of a major tourney, marching girls before they go on parade, beauty contestants before they step on the catwalk.

Now why are all these people nervous? The usual answer is: fear of failure. That may be partly true. But I want to suggest a more important reason, and when you understand the source of your fear you will also see how easy it is to overcome it.

The Real Reason For
Speaker's Fright

The advice that follows is, I believe, the single most important thing that can be said to any timid speaker. *The reason why you are nervous is the thought of a lot of people staring at you*. Weeks before you are due to give your speech, you will be dreading the idea of standing before the collective gaze of all those people. And when you step, cringing, before your audience, you will feel overpowered by all those eyes centred on you. That's what makes your mouth dry up, that's what renders your face a stricken mask, that's what puts a horrifying, uncontrollable quiver in your voice.

Make no mistake. This is what platform fear really is: the speaker mentally cowering before his audience.

When a speaker finally overcomes this fear, what happens? Quite simply, he reverses the feeling of who is looking at whom. This is what you must do. Instead of being overcome by the thought of all those eyes boring in upon you, you must think of yourself giving out to your listeners. You must feel that it is you who is in control. You must stand, speak and gesture with authority. In the nicest meaning of the word, you must dominate your audience. You must feel that you are in command of your listeners and you must be aware that *potentially the audience is more nervous than you*. It is essential to believe that if, at any moment, you were to point to a member of the audience and ask a question, then that person would be the one doing the cowering, as attention suddenly is transferred to him.

Look beyond my words and imagine the speaking situation. If you are nervous when standing there, it is because you feel a forbidding force emanating from the audience and pressing upon you. Instead of thinking of the audience as the target of your speech, you think of yourself as the target of the audience's attention. The confident, experienced speaker reverses that situation. He instils in himself the positive attitude that he is giving out to the audience, that all the dynamism flows from him to them. He doesn't allow any room for the feeling that the audience is homing in on him.

Consider what happens when an experienced speaker loses confidence in full flight: he stumbles, flounders, and makes a hash of a potentially good speech. This has happened occasionally to me. What has gone wrong? I want to suggest that always the speaker has lost his attitude of giving out to the audience, and suddenly has come to feel the attention of the audience bearing upon him. When he stumbled in his speech, he panicked. Perhaps he forgot something important in his address and now can't keep his theme together. Perhaps he garbled a sentence or two, and in hastily trying to recover, only made things worse. Perhaps he has said something unintentionally funny and has been thrown into confusion by the sudden burst of laughter from the audience. Now in those circumstances there is no need for him to lose control. It is essential to pause and concentrate on what he will say next. If he panics, and thinks 'I'm making a fool of myself', his sudden self-awareness will destroy that essential idea that the audience is the target of his speech; he will be thinking of himself as the target of the audience's attention.

Two Infallible Ways of Overcoming Your Nervousness

Now we have established that platform fear is caused by the feeling of people looking at you, we can see where the cure lies.

To overcome your nervousness, all you have to do is stop people looking at you.

Now, you may think that's impossible. There you are, standing on a raised dais before a hundred people who have all come to hear you, and who are waiting for you to speak. Of course they are looking at you. How could you possibly stop them?

Actually, it's often no problem at all.

Let's suppose your subject is gang violence. You can begin with these words: 'Ladies and gentlemen, I'd like to start with a question. How many of you are worried about the level of violence in our community?' Slowly some hands will go up. Then you point to one person and say: 'The man in the green jacket — what kinds of violence bother you?'

Immediately all eyes in the audience will swerve to the man in the green jacket. No longer will they be looking at you. Instead, it's the poor fellow in the green jacket who will have become the nervous centre of everyone's attention. You have uttered only two sentences — yet you have released some of the pressure that causes your anxiety.

Once the man in the green jacket has answered, point to someone else: 'The lady in the blue dress — what is it that bothers you about violence in our society today?'

This can go on for quite some time. You may pause at one point and say: 'There have been several suggestions that horsewhipping is the only cure for gang violence. Is there anyone who feels that may only worsen the problem?'

By now you will have done two clever things. You will have reduced or eliminated your nervousness, and you will have achieved audience involvement in your subject.

There are other ways to stop people looking at you. Bring along a chart and set it up on an easel *some distance from where you will be standing*. Then open your speech by asking people to look at the chart. That way you can chat quite happily about the information on the chart, secure in the knowledge that the audience is looking at the chart, not at you.

There are other visual aids you can use in the same way. If your subject is fire safety, you can bring along a charred heater that caused a fire and set it on a table some distance from you. Then begin your speech: 'I want you all to look at that heater over there . . .'

I have often seen a timid speaker lurch wretchedly through half his address, then point to a chart or visual aid, and suddenly become relaxed and confident as the audience switches its attention away from him. By accident he has discovered how to ease his nervousness.

Here then are two infallible ways of overcoming speaker's fright. All you have to do is transfer your listeners' attention from yourself to: (a) someone in the audience; (b) an object or chart you bring with you. These techniques solve the problem of platform fear by removing its cause — that's what makes them work so well.

Use these techniques, or variations on them, at the outset of your speech. They will relax you immediately, and there's a good chance you will remain relaxed when finally the audience transfers its gaze back to you. Once you have overcome your opening nerves, and have become absorbed in what you have to say, it is unlikely panic will return.

What Happens To Your Body When You Are Afraid?

So far, so good. One way of conquering your nervousness is to divert the audience's attention from you long enough to get settled in.

But this isn't always sufficient. It may not prevent you spending a miserable few days anticipating the event. It may not soothe the turmoil in your breast as you drive to the function, or prevent you telegraphing your anxiety to those you chat with before the proceedings begin.

So you need another way of overcoming your tensions. You need a way of suppressing the palpitations of your heart, easing the constrictions of your chest, bringing your voice under control.

To do this, you need to understand what happens to your body when you are afraid. Your mouth dries up (some speakers take un- believable amounts of water), your hands perspire (always carry a big handkerchief), the adrenalin gushes in your veins, your heart beats faster, your contracting stomach muscles rob you of all interest in food (though an hour later, after the speech, you will be ravenous), your legs tremble, your voice becomes strained, you want to go frequently to the toilet. Your body is responding to the anxiety signals from your brain. Drawing on deep primal instincts,

11

it is preparing itself for the challenge to come, a challenge that it will meet by combat or flight. And if the symptoms are extreme, it means your body is more intent on flight than on combat!

It is important to understand the extent to which your body may take control of you. That's most often apparent at the end of a function, when the speaker mingles with officials and crowd. Many speakers undergo such a release of tension at this point that they become almost euphoric. They can become super-talkative, babbling away on a 'high' produced by the adrenalin their system has worked up.

In order to deal with these bodily symptoms of fear, you have two things to do:

1. convince yourself that the challenge is not a matter of life and death, and therefore does not require that marshalling of forces which once was required for hand-to-hand combat or panic-stricken flight;

2. don't starve yourself of air by shallow breathing, as this will only intensify your body's efforts to draw more oxygen to your muscles, thus greatly increasing your general agitation.

It is important not to give exaggerated distress signals to your body. If you let your body believe it will soon have to confront raging beasts, it will rush into a state of alarm in which calm, assured speech will be out of the question.

First, convince yourself you are going to give an ordinary speech. Don't aim for a brilliant oration; don't try to out-joke Bob Hope; don't aspire to a standing ovation. You're a beginner, and all you're trying to do is a satisfactory job.

Second, remember all the boring, badly constructed speeches you have listened to. That, regrettably, is the norm. All you have to do is to be slightly better than that, and your audience will be grateful – especially if you keep it brief.

Third, the worst that can happen is that you will be as boring and as disjointed as many other speakers – and *that's* not something to get agitated about or to lose sleep over.

Fourth, human memory for the spoken word is extremely short – especially if the spoken word is boring and uninteresting. So even if you make a hash of things, people will have forgotten your speech within hours – certainly by the next day. It's only remarkable speeches that are remembered. Ordinary ones are quickly forgotten.

Once you have convinced yourself that even the possibility of giving a bad speech is nothing to stew over, you can concentrate on making it quite a good speech. Not brilliant (remember you're only a beginner) but still quite good. You will then communicate less stress to your body, and it will be less likely to over-react by flinging itself into uncontrollable agitation.

But don't place difficult burdens on your body. If you are keyed up, your body will want to carry more oxygen to your muscles and your brain. So don't reduce the supply of oxygen – increase it.

This is very important. Nervous speakers nearly always breathe shallowly and suffer partial oxygen starvation as a result. Driving to the venue, you hunch over the wheel, cramping your chest, lungs and throat. When you get to the hall your nervousness causes you to cringe slightly, lowering your head and rounding your shoulders. All of this restricts your breathing.

It has been known for hundreds of years that deep breathing reduces tension. And it is invaluable when you are feeling nervous. I suggest you build these steps into your preparation for public speaking.

At home, some time before you depart for your speaking engagement, take long, gulping breaths for five or ten minutes. Go outside and do some vigorous jogging or exercises to drag deep draughts of fresh air into your lungs. Run through part of your speech, orating to your rose garden if you wish, at full volume. If the neighbours look over the fence, wave to them and ask what they think of your address.

If you can, leave home fifteen or twenty minutes early and park your car several blocks from the hall where you are to speak. Walk briskly those few blocks, head erect, breathing very deeply and expanding your chest to the full. Think of your speech as you go. This is one of the most invigorating and stimulating preparations possible: the act of walking also helps to fix the form of your speech in your memory.

At the hall, continue to breathe deeply and slowly – though not as deeply as on your walk, or else you will seem like an expiring fish. You mustn't lapse into shallow breathing. So keep your head erect, smile, and chat with your hosts, breathing as slowly and as fully as you can.

Continue to watch your breathing right up to the time when your speech is due to begin. Then stand slowly. Keep your hand movements slow and deliberate. Smile. Keep smiling. Let your eyes rove over the audience. Don't hurry. Hasty, jerky movements can destroy your calm. Remember to pause at the outset. And to keep pausing from time to time. Above all, don't let your breathing become quick and shallow.

With most speakers (but not all) nervousness largely evaporates after they have been speaking a little while. The worst part is the very beginning of the speech, and I have now given you a number of techniques to help you get through that period.

It is true that some speakers 'forget their place' halfway through, and panic. Part of platform nervousness is the fear of forgetting – and again, there are techniques you can learn.

For about fifteen years I have been giving over a hundred speeches a year, of one kind or another. These days I am never overcome by nervousness, though I do get keyed up, especially when beginning a really important speech. But I well remember my misery when I started out. My first speech at the Imps speaking club required me to speak for a bare fifteen seconds and say who I was. I only just made it, my knees clattering like castanets. I wish that I knew then the simple techniques I have since seen work so well for others.

Knowing What To Expect
Greatly Eases Your Fears

I once knew an extremely capable woman who stuttered uncontrollably during normal conversation, but enunciated clearly when delivering her speeches. When lecturing, she knew exactly what she was going to say because she was always thoroughly prepared.

Later we will discuss the importance of thorough preparation, of travelling a hundred miles in your research for every mile of your speech. Thorough preparation gives you confidence because *you know what things will be like on the day itself.*

Knowing what to expect, knowing what things will be like, is of utmost importance, not only in easing your fears but also in ensuring that no disasters will occur.

The familiar situation is always less forbidding than the one you have never met before. Yet it amazes me how many speakers never ask the simplest questions about what they can expect on the day itself.

You need to know roughly how many people will be in the audience; whether they will be all male, all female, or mixed; their age group, and especially whether there will be any children or teenagers. You need to know the time of day; whether you are to speak first or last; how long you are to speak for; whether there will be questions from the audience. You need to know how well informed the audience is; whether they have any prejudices or strong political or social beliefs; and how much they are likely to know about your subject. Even knowing the venue can be a big help in preparing yourself.

Controlling Your Nervousness
In One-To-One Situations

Diverting the audience's attention is a marvellous way of reducing your fear. But you can't always do this. If you are being interviewed for a job or presenting a report to the board, or talking on television – you can hardly begin by asking, 'Hands up all those who . . .'

Let's suppose the phone rings at work. It's your boss. Not your immediate boss but the head of the firm, to whom you rarely speak. He asks to see you, but doesn't say what it is about. You put down the phone. Your heart is suddenly beating very fast. You know that by the time you reach his office you will be shaking with nervousness. What can you do?

Don't panic. Remember the advice given earlier. Collect your thoughts, and don't become over-anxious. Tell yourself you are not going to be brilliant: you are going to deal with the situation with reasonable competence. You are going to *concentrate*. You are going to think about the subject matter and not about the situation you are in. Keep a good control on your breathing. Don't allow your breath to come in quick, shallow bursts – keep it slow and deep.

As we proceed through the following chapters, you will learn more techniques that will make you much more confident and comfortable in any speaking situation.

I have spent much time discussing speaker's fright, because I know how important it is. You will soon get over your nervousness. Practise. Accept every opportunity to speak that is offered you. And keep coming back to this chapter for help. In return, I ask only one thing of you: pass on my advice to every nervous speaker you meet. Tell him or her of your own experiences and help him or her believe that anyone can become a confident speaker.

Summary

1. Don't expect to eliminate speaker's fright, simply to bring it under control. Being a little bit keyed up always makes for a better speech.

2. Being nervous about speaking in public is very natural, and extremely common.

3. Prepare carefully. Knowing what to expect will reduce your nervousness.

4. Deep breathing and relaxation exercises are very helpful.

5. Aim for competence, nothing more.

6. Remember that if you do, in the end, perform badly, you will be no worse than many other speakers.

7. Concentrate on your topic, not on being in front of an audience.

8. If other techniques do not work, distract the attention of the audience from yourself.

9. Think of giving out to the audience and (in a nice way) dominating them.

Chapter Two

HOW TO RESEARCH AND
BUILD YOUR SPEECH

What is it that gives a speech structure, cohesion, consistency – that sense of carrying the audience on a well-planned journey and of depositing them indisputably at the right destination? How do you avoid side-excursions, back-trackings, random collisions with irrelevancy?

In this chapter we will discuss how to plan and build your speech; how to research it; the different types of beginning; ways of leading your audience on; and how to wind it all up with a memorable ending.

Remember: a speech is not a regurgitation of someone else's views read from a book. It is *your* theme, *your* argument, formed out of your past experiences and the knowledge gained from your research, all welded together by thinking, arguing, reconsidering, shaping, unpicking, reworking. When complete, your speech will be a new creation, something that never existed before; it will reflect your personality, your attitudes, your view of life.

What Will Be The Purpose
Of Your Speech?

Whether your subject is suggested by the organisers or chosen by you, it will have a purpose. That purpose will be one of these:

1. To *inform* or *entertain* your audience, telling them: how to knit with fencing wire; what to expect from the new tax laws; how to train for the marathon; what it is like to hitchhike through Turkey.

2. To *persuade* them to accept a judgement or belief: that Adolf Hitler was misunderstood; that your firm should begin advertising on television; that chewing tobacco will prevent lung cancer; that the state should pay greater subsidies to the elderly.

3. To *motivate* them to action: to vote for you in the coming elections; to oppose the new motorway; to lose weight by thinking

thin; to support a new charity.

4. To get a *decision* on the spot: to obtain signatures on a petition; to take orders for your revolutionary macrame tennis racquet; to sign up new members of your club or church; to obtain a resolution to go on strike for better pay.

5. To perform a *social duty* on their behalf: to open a function; to congratulate someone; to introduce a speaker; to thank someone; to farewell someone; to be master of ceremonies. Social speeches are dealt with in Chapter 7; humorous speeches in Chapter 4; here we will deal with speeches designed to inform, persuade or motivate.

What Will Be The Theme
of Your Speech?

The *purpose* of your speech is the effect you hope to have on your audience. The *theme* of your speech is its message.

Many people bash their brains for days looking for a theme. Here's an easy way to shorten your search: your theme, or message, involves a judgement about your subject, and you will find that only three types of judgement can ever be made about it:

1. Everything about your subject is good (e.g. 'My Favourite Music').

2. Everything about your subject is bad (e.g. 'The Increase In Child Abuse').

3. Some things about your subject are good and some are bad (e.g. 'The Proposal To Build A Casino In Our City').

Commonly, subjects are of the third type. Your job is to weigh up the good and the bad, and to decide which way the balance tips. Often these are highly controversial topics: some people feel the balance tips one way (the revenue to the state and the boost to tourism from a casino outweigh any disadvantages) while others feel it tips the other way (no amount of tourism and tax revenue can outweigh the bad effects of gambling and an undesirable clientele).

Don't shy away from subjects of this kind. Though you may have difficulty deciding which way the balance tips, these are inherently dramatic subjects. As every novelist will tell you, conflict creates interest. So don't play down the tension between good and bad: highlight it, counterpoint it, and present your own conclusion.

By deciding whether your subject is type 1, 2 or 3, you will be able to concentrate and target your research. Where your theme is not already laid down for you (or determined by your prejudices), strike a tentative theme at the outset, and do your preparation with an open mind. Be ready to modify your theme, even abandon it, should the facts demand this.

Those First Tentative
Ideas and Jottings

From close questioning of the organisers you will know what sort of speech they hope for; what sort of audience you will confront; what subject you will deal with; how well informed your audience will be; what other speakers will cover. You will have thought about the purpose of your speech, and devised a tentative theme. Possibly you will have worked out a rough structure that fits your allotted time.

Next, interview yourself. Jot down everything you can think of on the subject. Use Kipling's 'six honest serving men': Who, What, When, How, Where and Why. What exactly is the problem you will speak about? For whom is it a problem? Where does the problem occur? When does it happen? Why is it a problem? How does it manifest itself? And so on.

Carry your jottings with you; take them out in the bus or during a pause in your weeding of the garden. Keep thinking of your subject while showering or feeding the baby. Discuss it with friends and colleagues. And add to your jottings.

Such mind-dredging produces surprising results. An early panic that you might have nothing to say gives way to a confident, eager arrangement and rearrangement of ideas. Many of your first thoughts will be of little value: abandon them when you rewrite your notes. Keep on rewriting and rearranging.

Plunging Into
Your Research

Your purpose has been established, and you have begun to work out a theme. Your first ideas are simmering in your head. Now you need some information. It is time for research.

Begin with libraries – not just the public library, but specialist libraries too. Every government department has one, and every major firm, every trade and professional association, every university, research organisation, welfare body and foreign embassy.

Don't read everything in sight. Seek the help of the librarian. Identify likely books by their titles; then skim the contents page and index; riffle through the pages; and abandon everything that looks unpromising.

Similarly, don't waste time poring through newspapers and magazines. Ring the newspaper's library, or, better still, contact a specialist reporter who covers your subject. For magazines, the public library should have the *Reader's Guide to Contemporary Literature,* which lists all significant articles in major periodicals, under subject headings.

Of course, never neglect the files at your place of work, if they hold appropriate information – and your firm's library if it has one.

Equally valuable are the experts in your subject. They compile files, write unpublished reports, clip newspaper and magazine articles, collect manuscript copies of other people's unpublished speeches – and store vast amounts of information in their heads.

On a controversial issue, go to anyone who is outspoken on the subject, whose interests are very much affected, or who is likely to have strong views about change. These include commercial organisations, consumer groups, environmentalists, civil liberties groups, lobbyists and pressure groups, trade unions, and the research units of political parties. People in teaching, research, government and journalism are ideal informants if you choose well.

It's best to ring first with a few exploratory questions to find out if an interview will be worthwhile – if not, seek the name of another person in the same organisation.

Don't be afraid to beard important people in their dens: politicians, chief executives of major firms, heads of government departments, the mayor, a professor at the university. At worst you will be turned away. But sometimes you will get to the eminent person himself – or failing that, to a lieutenant who may be as good or better. Remember, however, that busy people simply may not have time to talk to you. Don't press so hard for an interview that you become a nuisance.

Equally, you should be ruthless with your own time. If an interview is not producing useful information, cut it short. But never leave any interview without asking for names of other people or organisations knowledgeable about the subject. Above all, don't be swayed by unsupported opinion. Often people you interview will wax eloquent on their pet theories. That's fine, but press them for specifics – for hard facts to support their arguments.

Putting It All
Together

You may build your speech however you think best. But it will help you to be familiar with some common structures:

Time sequence: life of a person; history of a company; events of a journey; development of an idea; growth of an industry.

Work forward from the beginning through to the present. But be sure to identify and highlight conflict: challenges met and overcome; successes and failures; moral dilemmas confronted; mistakes made; triumphs of good judgement; defeat of opponents. And build in your theme: of commitment to excellence; of triumph over adversity; of refusal to accept conventional wisdom; of a clash of cultures; of the battle of a small organisation against the giants.

Problem-solving: how to grow roses in a cold climate; how paraplegics can learn to drive a modified vehicle; how to boost sales during an economic slump; how to prevent the mayor from ruining the city's finances.

It is usual to begin with the nature of the problem, then examine possible remedies, showing the weaknesses of those you deem inadequate, and building up the strengths of the solution you propose.

Taking sides in a dispute: arguing that abortion should be available on demand; that there should be a shift from direct to indirect taxes; that amateur sportspeople should not accept appearance money; that union representatives should be given places on the boards of major companies.

On any contentious issue, you will either propose a change, or defend the present situation. If you are *proposing change,* you will: (a) paint a picture of what is wrong; (b) show things are so bad they must be changed; (c) demonstrate that your solution will solve the problems; and (d) show that no other solution would be preferable. If you are *defending* the present situation, you will: argue either (a) that the defects in the present situation are not as bad as they are painted; or (b) that the proposed solution would introduce greater problems than it would solve. Whatever your stance, you will recognise, and rebut, the arguments of your opponents.

Making a judgement: that Bach was the greatest composer of all time; that the government is trigger-happy in its foreign affairs; that pre-marital sex is wrong.

Usually you will start by setting out persuasively the criteria for making your judgement; then you will show that the criteria are met in the present case. Throughout, you seek to establish the reason why people should accept your judgement. Again, you must recognise opposing points of view and refute them.

Your first speech will probably be written out in full, and you will read it to your audience word for word. Later, as you become more skilled, you will jot down brief notes or trigger words on small cards and speak from them.

Beginnings: You Must
Get Attention

Novices tend to think that their speech will begin with the title or first sentence. Not so. Your speech will begin with you sitting next to the chairman and being introduced by him. That is the first impression of you the audience will get. Will you seem stiff or nervous? Or will you be so relaxed that when the chairman pauses during his laudatory remarks, you will call out jovially: 'That sounds as though it was written by my mother!'

The first words you utter will often be *Mr Chairman* or *Mr Chairperson,* or *Madame Chairwoman* or *Madame Chairperson.* The commonest salutations are:
– *Mr Chairman, ladies and gentlemen* . . .
– *Mr Chairman and gentlemen* . . .
– *Madame Chairwoman and ladies* . . .
– *Mr Chairperson, ladies and gentlemen, boys and girls* . . .
Sometimes the salutation is informal: *Mr Chairman and friends.* Or even: *Chairperson Betty and friends.*

If important people are present, it is best to clump them together: *Mr Chairman, distinguished guests, ladies and gentlemen.* Try not to go into a catalogue of notables: it is boring, and you may get the pecking order wrong. The list of titles in any community is forbiddingly long, and the order of precedence complex. If you must list them separately, consult an appropriate book on precedence in your local library.

Sometimes it is essential to mention a person by name: a visiting cabinet minister, or the general manager of your firm. Thus: *Mr Chairman, the Honourable Mrs Votecatcher, ladies and gentlemen*. Note that the chairman or chairwoman is always mentioned first, except when royalty is present.

These opening words may launch you straight into your speech. But often not. Many speakers begin with a short preamble that has nothing whatever to do with the content of the speech to follow. (While salutations usually form your first words, it is quite permissible to open with a preamble, then use the salutations to start the speech itself.) The preamble can pick up a statement made by the chairman or preceding speaker; or bring greetings from a rival club to which you belong; or refer to a previous speech you made to this group; or tell them your father once belonged to their number; or pick up a reference in the morning newspaper that affects them all. A preamble is often used where the audience is likely to be hostile to the speaker or his message. It is part of the softening-up tactics (as we will see in the next chapter).

Here are some common beginnings:
1. The softening-up preamble (e.g. shared experience) that seeks to get the audience on side.
2. A piece of relevant humour that eases into your main theme.
3. A teasing or tantalising promise of much interest to come.
4. A verbal picture or story or anecdote to enliven what otherwise would be a flat description.
5. A piece of personal experience.
6. A dramatic statement or quotation as your opening remark.
7. A comment on a topical issue or recent development that affects your audience.
8. An historical reference (which must be lively, engaging and relevant to your theme).

Whatever you do, the opening of the speech proper must get attention. Never, never begin 'My subject tonight is . . .'. They already know that. It's been advertised, and the chairman mentioned it in his introductory remarks.

You must grab the audience at the start. Build high promise. Create suspense; or curiosity; tease them; shock them; amuse them. Remember the basic formula of all radio and television serials: make them cry, make them laugh, make them wait. Especially, *make them wait*. Dangle in front of them the prospect of fascinating or scandalous or revolutionary information to follow. Tie that information to what interests them.

Nowhere else do you have better opportunity to make them wait. Titillate them at the beginning and you will have their thoughts on a string thereafter. Consider this opening:

These are dark days, desperate days, for this club. At the end of this season we could be relegated to the second division in the competition. Our performance is that bad. And there is Blue Sox leading us all by a mile. But what everyone tends to forget is that seven years ago Blue Sox was at the bottom of the competition. Why? They were making the same mistakes as we are making now. Tonight I want to describe those mistakes and to show that we can overcome them in the same way as Blue Sox did. But it won't take us seven years. We can be back on top at the end of this season if we do everything right.

Pause. The speaker can let that pause lengthen to eight or ten seconds while he surveys the expectant audience. He won't lose their concentration. They won't talk to each other, shift in their seats, look at the floor, scratch themselves. He's got them. He's using the tactics of a gossip who telephones a friend and says breathlessly: 'I've got the most amazing thing to tell you about Georgina. But I wouldn't dare to say it on the phone. You'll have to come over.'

The promise-of-what's-to-come opening is always a sure attention-getter if your theme revolves around facts or ideas that are of great interest or benefit to your listeners: if you are going to tell them how to achieve something they desire (beating Blue Sox in the competition) or how to avoid something they dread (being relegated to the second division).

Painting a picture (or telling a story) is always a good evocative opening, especially if you base it on personal experience:

When I was a boy, the school tuckshop made most marvellous meat pies. They put real chunks of meat in them, not this synthetic junk we get today. And peas and carrots and potatoes. One of those delicious, gravy-rich pies would cost me two cents, handed piping hot across the counter wrapped in a square of greaseproof paper. How well I remember that dreadful day when the price went up to three cents in one appalling 50 per cent jump. My parents, who were poor, were forced to reduce the frequency of my pie purchases by half. Later the price of a pie jarred upward another two cents, but this time, though the increase was two-thirds rather than one half, I suffered less distress – maybe because I was getting used to the idea of inflation.

Well, over the last forty years I have watched the price of a meat pie rise steadily from two cents until now it is 70 cents. For me, that's the measure of inflation: The way the price of a meat pie has risen, and the way the quality has dropped — because some of them today taste as if they were made by a carpet manufacturer.

Now isn't that a far better way of beginning a speech on inflation than by quoting what has happened to the consumers price index in a welter of figures, dates and percentages? It is personal and vivid, and it compels belief because it comes from the speaker's own experience.

Middles: The Secret
Is To Lead Them on

There would never again be a boring address if speakers followed this maxim: lead them on. That's exactly what a good story-teller does. He builds a sequence of events, linking one to the next, making full use of suspense, curiosity and mystery. If a good story-teller is interrupted, the audience will be left fretting and wondering: how did it end; what was he leading up to? So too with a speaker: if an outbreak of fire cuts him short, his audience should feel deprived for some time after.

Some speakers flop at the very start: by apologising for their inexperience; by baldly reciting the title of their address; by taking too long to get into the pith of their speech. As they progress, they may make a worse mistake by stating their opinions with insufficient evidence. Facts are skated over lightly, instead of being built up convincingly. The audience becomes quickly bored because they are not *led on*.

Good structure depends on:
1. A clear definition of the issue.
2. A line of argument; a theme; a purpose.
3. A careful selection of the most telling examples, or pieces of evidence, to support your theme.
4. The building up, or teasing out, of those examples so that their full import becomes clear. Dramatise your evidence; show its relevance for your theme; paint pictures with it.
5. The recognition of opposing points of view, and rebuttal of them.
6. A tidy conclusion that draws everything together persuasively.

Remember: be selective. Keep your main line of argument as simple as possible. Choose only the most telling pieces of evidence. Devote time to establish a few pieces of evidence; don't hurl a welter of ill-digested facts at your audience. In particular, develop pieces of evidence that counter the main objections that can be raised to your argument.

Your speech must develop momentum logically – progressing inexorably towards a firm and clear conclusion. Let it move forward by means of evidence and argument. Evidence is facts. Argument is how you use those facts to establish a conclusion. As we will see in the final chapters on debating, a common fault in speeches of all kinds is too much argument and insufficient evidence. Strong, compelling facts are the reinforcing rods that give strength to a good speech.

You must avoid vague generalisations in your speech; people respond to *specifics,* to hard facts, statistics, your own experiences, the experiences of others, what experts have found. So most of your preparation must be a search for the facts that will support your tentative conclusion (or theme) or change it to a more sound conclusion.

Endings: Wind It All Up
With A Stirring Finish

If you have focused your message, clarified your purpose, and streamlined the structure of your argument, you will find the end comes naturally. It is not a question of knowing when and how to stop. It is a question of travelling a planned route and arriving at a pre-determined destination — finish. When you reach your note cards, the trigger words thereon will lead you into a carefully rehearsed ending.

Of course, you will never telegraph that you are approaching finality. It is particularly lame to use such winding-down expressions as:
- *In conclusion* . . .
- *I am afraid I have gone on rather long* . . .
- *I am just about at the end* . . .
- *My final point is* . . .
- *If you will bear with me a little longer* . . .

Under no circumstances should you tail off into a fumbling

'Thank you for listening to me' (it's *their* job to thank *you*, with applause). Nor will you apologise for long-windedness, inexperience, or inadequate knowledge of the subject. That ruins any climax.

Using eye contact, pausation and full modulation of voice, end your speech with as much control and intensity as you began. Hit them with your last stirring statement; pause; survey them one final time; then go back to your seat.

Most often, your conclusion will be a powerful restatement of your theme, usually in heightened or dramatised form. Or it may be:
1. A summary of your most telling points.
2. A call for action, for people to buy your product, support your cause, fight a common enemy, solve a problem, adopt a principle.
3. An apt quotation or humorous story or anecdote that illustrates your message.
4. A request that those gathered should drink a toast, applaud, or burst into song.
5. An expression of thanks, good wishes, congratulations or gratitude.
6. The resolution of a mystery or puzzle you have built up, or grappled with, in your speech.

Remember: episodic, sprawling, badly-structured speeches are difficult to bring to a close. You will be tempted to keep on introducing new facts or opinions; or to drag in some inconsequential point at the last minute.

If you get your structure right, you will get your ending right. Above all, plan the exact words of your last 'paragraph' and rehearse them as carefully as your opening. Then when you hit that last paragraph you will be at your destination.

Summary

1. Find out about your audience.

2. Range widely in your research.

3. Fix a tentative theme; build evidence and argument around it.

4. Get attention at the outset; then lead the audience on.

5. Select the most telling examples and build them up, relating them to your theme.

6. Weed out irrelevant material and argument.

7. Recognise opposing points of view and rebut them.

8. Prepare and rehearse the ending as thoroughly as you do your beginning.

9. Wind it all up with a stirring finish.

Chapter Three

HOW TO WIN OVER A HOSTILE AUDIENCE

When an audience is listening to you, its members are thinking *Yes* or *No* or *Maybe*. If from the outset they begin thinking a resolute *No,* you may as well go home. That stubborn, jaw-set negative is unlikely ever to melt. Your jokes will collapse painfully; your questions will produce little response; your message will never reach them; and in question time they may well set upon you.

Your task is to get them thinking *Yes* from the start. Or if that is not possible, to get them thinking *Maybe;* then work to turn that *Maybe* into a *Yes* or at least an open mind on your proposals.

Hostile audiences are of two kinds:

1. Those who are hostile to you before you begin, because they already know and dislike your views, or because they know the organisation you represent, and have a strong aversion to it.

2. Those who become hostile because of what you say, or how you say it.

Hostility need not be of the raucous, heckling variety. It may simply be a stony unwillingness to accept your views or your manner of presenting them. You may suffer no abuse nor even overt unfriendliness – you will simply fail to get your message across.

In this chapter I want to discuss the art of persuasion – of giving your opinions the best opportunity of being accepted by your audience. We will look at ways in which you can ruin your chances from the start by adopting the wrong tactics or the wrong tone; we will examine methods of letting your message form gradually in the minds of your listeners so that it seems more their idea than yours; we will examine ways of combating the fixed beliefs of your listeners; we will look at the tactics you can use in the question and answer period; and (for the occasions where all else fails) we will discuss how to handle hecklers and other disrupters.

When Your Audience Dislikes You In Advance

An audience that dislikes you, or your views, or the organisation you represent, will be putting up barriers even before you begin to speak. You must start by dismantling some of these. As director of a consumer protection organisation, I have made hundreds of speeches to audiences opposed to my message: groups of bankers, lawyers, manufacturers, retailers, dentists, importers, wholesalers, advertising agencies, and so on. Almost always, I have used a short preamble to loosen them up, before easing into my theme.

It is often a good idea to acknowledge your unpopularity at the outset. Once I set out to persuade a group of executives of electricity supply authorities that they should amalgamate into larger and more efficient units – a proposal that was anathema to them. I began my address thus:

This morning I left my home in Wellington before dawn. When I arrived at the airport it was still dark. The place was virtually deserted. After checking in I strolled down the corridor, puzzled that I could see no other passengers. I climbed the steps and took a seat in the empty aircraft, beginning to wonder if some mistake had been made. Then an air hostess appeared. 'Where are all the other passengers?' I asked. She shrugged and said: 'You are it.' So I sat there alone thinking to myself: 'I know I am unpopular . . . but this is ridiculous!'

The audience loved it. I followed with more cracks about my unpopularity, watching them relax as I did so. When I eased into my speech proper, I knew I had dissolved much of the bristling hostility with which the meeting had begun.

On another occasion I addressed a group of lawyers who knew I would urge more price competition upon them and condemn their anti-competitive scale of fees. They were aware that I am not a lawyer, so my opening words immediately struck a chord:

'This morning I expect all of you to address me as "My learned friend" ', I said.

Smiles blossomed.

'That is because I have just become one of you,' I added.

The smiles changed to puzzled frowns.

'Recently I was appointed a member of the Law Society's Future Planning Committee.' Their expressions changed to astonishment.

'And if you want to know what idiot put me on your planning committee, it was your national president, Bruce Slane.'

They enjoyed that. So I followed quickly with my punchline: 'And if you want to know *why* I was put on the planning committee, well, I did overhear Bruce Slane saying: "I wanted to put the little sod where I could keep an eye on him." '

The audience whooped. Here was a speaker both poking fun at himself and participating in their affairs. This preamble uses two of the fundamental rules on the use of humour: make yourself the butt of your joke, and weave in shared experience (see Chapter 4).

Shared experience is especially effective in establishing rapport with your audience. It helps to make you one of them, less of an outsider. You may pick up items of common experience in discussion before you speak, or from the comments of speakers who precede you. But it is wise to do research first, so that facts about the organisation you are addressing can be woven into your preamble or the speech itself. Remember to be specific, not general, in your comments, especially where you are giving praise. It can sound insincere and ingratiating if you begin: 'I've always been most impressed with the way your club helps out in the community.' Far better to open:

Twenty-three thousand four hundred and twelve dollars! I bet all of you will remember that figure for years. And I bet you will remember the sweat that went into earning it. And all those Saturdays of giving up golf and basketball and tennis to push wheelbarrows and paint roofs and trim hedges and dispose of refuse. But it was worth it, wasn't it? Now the physically handicapped kids have a specially equipped vehicle for their outings. When I saw that photograph in the newspaper of your President, Margot Fox, handing over the keys of the vehicle, I had to smile. She was grinning like a big kid herself . .

Notice that your praise is indirect. By recounting, with warmth, the details of the club's community exercise, you show how much you appreciate and admire their efforts. They will like it too that you went to the trouble of getting all the details.

The right time for praise is early in your speech, before you come to the part they may not like. Beginning with hard-hitting criticism and ending with what you hope is balancing praise will simply produce a *No* response from the start. The praise will seem an insincere afterthought.

31

How Not To Get Offside
With Your Listeners

Now let's look at a different type of speech. Here the audience has no pre-conceived ideas about you. But you know, nonetheless, that your theme is one they are likely to find unpalatable. Again, it is advisable to use a preamble before starting the speech proper: shared experience, relevant humour, genuine praise full of specifics, a jab at a common enemy, some self-mocking remarks about your alleged deficiencies.

In this way, you seek to have your listeners warm to you from the beginning, to get them thinking at least *Maybe,* or hopefully *Yes.* But having got them onside, be careful not to ruin the effect.

First, watch the tone you use. Don't become hectoring, officious, opinionated. Play yourself down. Don't patronise them. Don't flaunt your knowledge. Don't needle them, or provoke them. It is so easy, when you seem to be hitting it off with your audience, to become over-confident, aggressive and bumptious.

Be aware of the audience at all times. Be sympathetic, courteous, plausible, sincere. Above all, you must project warmth, sincerity and friendliness. Your pauses, the way you let their laughter subside before continuing, are all part of your responsiveness to them.

You will try to begin with a point they agree with, and you will try to tell them some things they want to hear. You will make a sly dig at a common enemy, flatter them with words of praise or congratulation that show a detailed understanding of their achievement.

In all of this you will be good-humoured, relaxed, unruffled by any early interjections. You will not be ingratiating or obsequious. Your job is not to fall into line with them, but to take them step by step to a conclusion you expect they will not like.

Right from the start, you will take care not to push your opinions upon them. You will avoid use of the word *I* as much as possible, substituting *we* and *you* wherever you can. Avoid assertion like the plague. Instead, show them your evidence, and lead them gently to your conclusion.

Let's suppose this is a group of employers, and you are going to argue that truck drivers should be paid more. If you simply state that opinion, perhaps belligerently daring them to disagree, you will turn them off. Barriers will go up, and they will all start thinking *No.* As you continue to assert that truck drivers and their families live below the breadline, that they are examples of sweated labour, that employers are exploiting the workers who make their profits possible, you may release a few of your frustrations but you will gain little sympathy from your audience.

Now compare this approach. After taking a few wry, humorous jabs at yourself, ease into your speech:

I want to tell you the story of a man named Andy. Andy has a wife and four children. His food bill alone comes to $86.50 a week. In winter, there's the added cost of heating. That's what makes winter such a bad time – the cost of heating the house all day. Andy's life is divided into fortnights, for that is his pay period. And each fortnight is divided into 14. That figure of 14 is a recurring twice-monthly nightmare for Andy. For by Day 11 his pay has begun to run out. Those last three days he finds unbearable. I want to describe them to you – Day 12, Day 13, Day 14 of every fortnight as lived by Andy and his family. That, gentlemen, is what my speech is about – Day 12, Day 13 and Day 14 for a family whose money always begins to run out on Day 11 . . .

To this point you haven't said Andy is a truck-driver. He might easily be caretaker at a cemetery, nothing to do with these employers at all. Nor have you said what he earns. Much less have you said you think he should earn more. Not until the very last paragraph of your speech will you mention *that*. For the next forty minutes you will play upon the heartstrings of those of them who have hearts. You will watch them squirm in their seats as you tease out the story of Day 12, Day 13 and Day 14. So far as you can, you will get your listeners to live those three days, hour by hour, and to understand what it is to face payday knowing that the next Day 12 is only eleven days away.

Well, of course even this may not convince such a hard-bitten crew. But if you do it well, you will send most of them away with a gnawing *Maybe* stirring within them. Be in no doubt: one of the greatest speaking skills is to refrain from belabouring your listeners. Far better to let them come slowly to a realisation that your argument is really very plausible. That's the art of diplomacy: letting the other fellow have your way. Your job, then, is not to assert the truth but to demonstrate it; not to tell your listeners but to show them; to illustrate, not flatly describe; to evoke feelings in your audience rather than demanding that they have such feelings.

You must learn to paint pictures with words.

Eight Ways To Weaken
Preconceived Ideas

We have seen that one way of combating the fixed beliefs of your listeners is to avoid meeting those beliefs head-on. Here are eight other ways in which you can approach an audience you expect to be hostile to your theme:

1. *Concede the merits of their case.* Many of the issues that divide the community are incapable of final resolution. There is no absolute right or wrong: only competing opinions and conflicting evidence. Where you have come down firmly on one side of such a dispute, it is fool-hardy, and unfair, to paint your opponents as idiots whose stance is devoid of merit. Far better to concede that they have persuasive arguments; then outline the force of the opposite point of view; and suggest that is the way the balance tips. By recognising the worth of the other person's viewpoint you increase the chances that he or she will be more receptive to yours. (See also Chapters 11 and 12 on debating skills.)

2. *Attack ideas, not people.* Sometimes you will feel your opponents have done or said something that cannot be excused, and about which you can say nothing kind. Your speech may, for example, flatly condemn the decision of a sporting club to exclude non-whites. Don't portray the club members as ogres; on the contrary, praise their past performances, their high standards, their successful community work. Make them feel good about themselves, and take time to demonstrate that your admiration is genuine. Then slowly, subtly, switch your emphasis: show how grave is the risk of their fine reputation being damaged; show how admission of non-whites might strengthen the club. If you really want to get them thinking *Maybe,* or perhaps a majority of them thinking *Yes,* don't attack them personally. Try to get them to see that they as good people have made a rare mistake in deciding to ban non-whites – a mistake that should now be rectified.

3. *Don't hesitate to shift the blame.* Sometimes the people with whom you seem to be in conflict are not really at fault. Let's suppose you are speaking to a group of bankers (or retailers) about the unintelligible wording of the documents they get their customers to sign. You have to realise a bank doesn't *want* to produce a mortgage

document containing a clause that is 524 words long without comma or fullstop. A retailer doesn't *want* his time-payment contract to be 'executed' rather than 'signed'; nor does he want it to 'determine' rather than 'end'. The archaic words and tortuous sentences are not sins of the firms that issue the agreements; they are sins of the lawyers who drew up the agreements.

So be sure of your real target. Butter your retailers up – give detailed and knowledgeable praise of the way they conduct most of their business. Then introduce the one aspect of their operation of which you are critical. Make clear at once that you recognise the fault does not lie with them. Demonstrate what is so wrong and unfair about the documents. Tell them you realise the problem is caused by the misguided wish of their lawyers to protect them. Ask them to go back to their lawyers and demand language their customers (and their staff) can readily understand. Show how other firms have persuaded their lawyers to do this, and have won the gratitude of their customers. If you do it right, you will send each of your listeners away ready to do battle with his lawyer. If you do it wrong (if you make your listeners think that they are to blame for their rotten agreements) you will probably not persuade them to change anything.

4. *Show them they have been misled*. This is one of the most potent devices you can use in attempting to dislodge the fixed opinions of an audience. Once again, you are not placing the blame on them. If you can show they have taken up a wrong position because of mistaken, incomplete, or biased information, you are well on the way to changing their minds. Often, they will become so angry at having been misled, that they will swing hard over to your point of view.

5. *Reveal new evidence*. This too is a very effective method of altering entrenched positions because it allows people to shift their ground without losing face.

The state of our knowledge has expanded rapidly in the past few years. Previously there was little firm evidence of the value of acupuncture, and its principles were in conflict with medical commonsense. But now thoroughly scientific tests have been done and the results are emphatic. Like you, I used to think acupuncture a load of oriental hogwash, but I have changed my mind, and I think you will too . . .

Here the strategy is to make them feel that their disbelief in acupuncture was based on good grounds and would have been shared by any sensible person possessing the same information, but that new information now gives them good reason to change their opinion.

6. *Use a parallel case.* This two-step strategy seeks to obtain the agreement of the audience to a principle outlined in a context in which they are bound to agree with it; then to use the same principle in a context where they are less likely to agree. If you can get a *Yes* response in a non-threatening situation, you may be able to transfer that *Yes* to a parallel situation. Let's suppose you are to give a speech against capital punishment and you suspect some of your listeners favour it. You could open with a discussion of a form of punishment still used in parts of the Middle East: severance of a hand for theft. Describe this horror in detail, and the often trivial nature of the crimes it is supposed to deter. Then say to your audience:

We all agree this practice is barbaric. None of us could describe exactly why. But we know in our bones, as human beings, that it is barbaric. Well, I want to shift now to a different form of punishment. I want to say to you, by analogy, that capital punishment is equally barbaric. I can't explain exactly why the death penalty is so inhuman (and so degrading to those who condone it), no more than I can explain why cutting off a hand for theft is inhuman and degrading. There is a twisted logic in saying that removing the hand that steals is just; and there is an equally perverse logic in saying that killing the man who kills is just . . .

The success of this stratagem will depend on how well you draw the analogy. If you can show your audience that the inhuman nature of the death penalty parallels punishment by amputation, you may well win them to your position.

7. *Demonstrate the weight of opinion on your side.* Though the majority are not always right, it is nonetheless useful if you can show all arrows pointing in the same direction. Begin your speech by describing how other countries implemented a proposal. Show the dire predictions of disaster did not come to pass, and that the benefits of the proposal were realised. Then go on to argue that your country should do the same, fine-tuning the proposal where neces-

sary in light of overseas experience. If you show effectively how the doom-sayers were proved wrong in other countries, you will greatly weaken the opposition of doom-sayers in your audience.

8. *Dangle a worse prospect before them*. This age-old ploy remains hugely effective today.

Already the environmentalists are proposing a new law to force all of you to control the pollutants you produce. And the Government is listening to them. So is the community. I urge you to act now; clean up your operation before you are compelled to do so. Just think how draconian the new law may be; imagine what it would be like with officious bureaucrats descending upon you in snap inspections to see whether you are complying. But if you get in first you can prevent the government poking its nose into yet another aspect of your business; and moreover you will restore your besmirched reputation and disarm your critics.

This manoeuvre works best when you spend the early part of your speech building up a 'worse prospect' in all its unwholesome detail, then switch to the prospect you favour, emphasising that it is moderate and reasonable and workable. Use this device adroitly, and you will convert the most obstinate opponent to your point of view. Again, the trick is to give him good reason for abandoning his entrenched opinion. Indeed, he can continue to proclaim the rightness of his original position, yet say he has 'no option' but to discard it.

Many audiences are set in their ways. Maybe their organisation has a longstanding policy that is the exact opposite of your message. If you do not prepare the way, then as your theme develops, and becomes apparent, their eyes will hurl double *Nos* at you from all round the room.

Yet, as we have seen, it need not be like that. The gentle art of persuasion – for gentle it surely is – gives you a variety of tactics to choose from. There are many ways of skinning a cat and quite the worst is to jab the poor beastie directly on the nose with the point of your knife. One of the great truths about public speaking is that persuasion is far, far more effective than browbeating; to persuade you must not merely put yourself in the other person's shoes, but wear them.

37

When The Organisers
Let You Down

When you face a hostile, or potentially hostile, audience the last thing you want is to have your carefully structured speech disrupted. Beware. Possibly half the people who organise speaking events are inept, and they have several ways of ruining your speech.

1. By asking you to cut it short when the programme gets behind time. This is because earlier speakers were permitted to go beyond their allotted span. Remedy: ask to go on first. Otherwise, insist that the chairman keep speakers to their time by using squares of paper marked '5 minutes', '3 minutes' and 'Please conclude'. Make sure every speaker understands that these notices will be placed in front of him as he starts to run over time. Be firm. If you cut your speech short and ruin it, the audience will not blame the earlier speakers for running on; they will blame you for a bad speech.

2. An after-dinner speaker will sometimes be brought on far too late – I have twice been announced after 11 p.m. (But never again – I will walk out long before.) Imagine: for two hours the diners have been drinking as if they were just in from the desert; half of them have been stomping to the danceband for an hour; then the chairman rises, waving his arms like some high priest, and intones 'Back to your seats everyone – I want to introduce our guest speaker.'

Be sure you discuss the timing and arrangements of the event with the organisers – and don't let them ruin the speech you have carefully prepared for this tricky audience.

That Daunting Question
And Answer Period

A speech is largely monologue. But the question and answer period at the end . . . ah, that is exhilarating dialogue. Yet inexperienced speakers who are nervous enough about the monologue become positively terrified at the thought of dialogue. This is a sad misconception. The question period should be the best and most enjoyable part, for it is then that you interact with your listeners and find out what they really want to know (as opposed to what you thought they wanted to know).

When given one hour, I always split it into 30 or 35 minutes for my speech, with 25 to 30 minutes for questions. Often the questions will go on much longer, and on a few thoroughly enjoyable occasions have lasted nearly two hours. Frequently, it is during this time I find I make most progress in changing the attitude of a hostile audience.

Don't collapse the end of your speech and slide anti-climactically into 'Are there any questions?' This unwisely raises the possibility that there may be none. Instead, finish your speech on a high note, then sit down. After the audience has stopped applauding, the chairman will rise and announce what you've primed him to say: 'Dick Smithies is very keen to answer questions. He asks me to tell you that there are no restrictions – he will try to answer anything you want to ask him.'

Don't stand until you hear the first question – in case there isn't one. Some speakers fear a ringing judgemental silence more than they dread the questions themselves. So they plant friends in the audience to bob up with benign questions and even complimentary remarks! That's plainly dishonest and unprofessional. It's also unnecessary, for you can drop invitations during your speech: 'I won't elaborate on this point but those who are interested can ask me for more information during question time.' Or, 'I'd like to hear your views on this aspect during question time.' Or, 'I can give you the name of a really good book on this subject if you care to ask me in question time.'

If the questions still come slowly, don't hesitate to stimulate them. 'Isn't someone going to ask how often I'm threatened with lawsuits for the sort of things I say?' Or, 'One question I am always asked is . . . Don't you people want to know the answer?' Or, 'Would you like to hear about the time one of our experiments blew up?' Or, 'Can I ask what was your reaction when I suggested . . .?'

It's a good idea to hold back humorous or startling information to liven the question period. You should always possess far more information about your subject than you have used in your speech. If you are capable only of delivering a prepared script, and not of enlarging upon it, you may as well send a tape recording – for the audience will not be able to bring out the real flavour of your message.

Later we will discuss the analytical techniques used by expert debaters (Chapters 11 and 12). Debaters spend as much time looking at their opponents' point of view as they do in shaping their own. If you do likewise in preparing your speech, you need have no fear of the question session. Question time is often a form of mini-debate, and a well-prepared speaker who understands definition, evidence, argument and rebuttal will cope handsomely with the most awkward questions.

What if you are asked something you cannot respond to? Say so. Be as frank, honest, sincere as in your main speech. But what if you are asked a whole series of questions you can't answer? Then you have to say something: 'I can't answer that, but your question does remind me of something else I left out . . .' Or, 'I'm not sure about that, but here's something I'd like to point out . . .'

Always, there is someone who asks a long, rambling question. There is one simple response to this (and it always brings a burst of laughter from the audience): 'Come on now, that isn't a question . . . it's a questionnaire!'

If you cannot understand what you are being asked, say politely, 'I'm sorry; I didn't follow that; can you re-phrase your question?'

Maybe you understand the question, but doubt the audience does. Your response: 'If I understand correctly, what you are asking is this . . . Am I right?'

When someone becomes angry and argumentative, just smile and reply: 'You are entitled to your opinion, but we're going to have to disagree. I stand by my position for the following reasons . . .'

Of course if a questioner makes a good point, don't hesitate to agree: 'You are quite right. I'd like to modify what I stated in my speech in the light of what you have just said.'

Remember: you are on trial whenever the questions are coming thick and fast. Above all, a keen audience will want to find out how good you are when under fire, and how honest you are in conceding points.

Remain unruffled, friendly, smiling and attentive. Don't sound impatient or defensive. Pause thoughtfully before answering: be concise, and don't allow yourself to ramble. Never patronise your questioners, nor try to put them down. Be sympathetic and courteous. Agree where you reasonably can. Where you cannot, show respect for the questioner's point of view.

If you have done a persuasive job in your main speech, and deal fairly and frankly with the audience in question time, your enemies may even turn into your friends!

How To Handle
Persistent Hecklers

Despite your best efforts to win over your audience, your speech may be disrupted by rowdies. Noisy and uncooperative audiences are all part of public speaking. There is no law that says your listeners must listen passively. If you bore them, they are entitled to shout, 'This is boring!' If you enrage them, they may protest. If they think you illogical, they may say so.

While some hecklers are garrulous pests, others can be devastatingly witty. They can destroy an unprepared speaker who assumes he is the unchallengeable guest of the gathering.

Experienced speakers do like to get responses from their audiences, and they feed off interjections. But beginners dread being taken on by a heckler. The usual advice is either 'ride over' the interjector, or deal with him briefly and effectively. If you plough on with your speech, hoping that a heckler will give up, he often will. If not, here are four devices you can use:

1. Disconcert her. Stop suddenly in mid-sentence, turn and stare wordlessly at her, your face clearly tinged with disdain. The audience (by now probably as fed up with her as you are) will turn to look at her too. Chances are she will scrunch down in her chair in embarrassment.

2. If just staring is not enough, you can use a rehearsed put-down. Be icily polite: 'Do be careful, Sir. If you open your mouth much wider you may swallow yourself . . . and die instantly of food poisoning.' You can work up any number of prepared rejoinders: 'Look, lady, I wish you would go off somewhere and gargle . . . with wet cement.' Or an appeal to the audience: 'That fellow in the plaid suit really ought to be out in the middle of the harbour somewhere . . . he sounds like a foghorn and he makes about as much sense.'

3. Pause, stare at the heckler, then say firmly, 'I'm glad to see you have strong views on this. You are the first person I will call on to speak from the floor at the end of my address.'

4. Most devastating of all is the on-the-spot rejoinder that answers and crushes the point the heckler is trying to make. It requires experience and some luck.

Persistent hecklers annoy the audience as much as they do you – so if you score off a heckler, the audience will be with you.

Of course, sometimes you will be met with a brilliant, unanswerable interjection. These are to be treasured. They are part of the cut and thrust of human communication. Just turn and face the interjector, give a beaming smile, and put your hands together in a small, soundless piece of applause. If you truly appreciate good use of language, never fail to salute an opponent who has squarely done you down.

On rare occasions even the most experienced speaker may face an audience he cannot control. Don't persevere. It is pointless shouting words that cannot be heard. Appeal to the chairperson, whose job it is to keep order. If he or she cannot calm the audience, or one or two vociferous members, he may decide to call the police to have the worst troublemakers ejected. Failing that, your speech will have to be abandoned.

Summary

1. Throughout your speech, the audience is thinking *Yes,* or *No,* or *Maybe.* At the end it should be *Yes.*

2. Use a softening-up preamble whenever your audience is hostile at the outset.

3. Praise must be specific and detailed.

4. Don't become over-confident and bumptious.

5. Try to let your message form gradually in their minds so that it seems more theirs than yours.

6. Use stealth to outwit hostile listeners.

7. Beware the organisers.

8. Try and enjoy question time: you can handle it!

9. Hecklers are tricky; work out some tricks of your own.

Chapter Four

HOW TO WRITE HUMOUR
AND MAKE IT WORK

There is probably only one kind of speech in which there should be no humour: a funeral oration. Nearly every other speech (formal or informal) will benefit from a little laughter. Occasionally you have to be very careful: if you are announcing a solemn event, such as the terms under which management and workers at your firm have settled a dispute, a jesting remark can be dangerous because it may be misconstrued.

I don't want to give the impression that all speeches must contain humour. This isn't so. Many of the most stimulating debates I have heard have been straightfaced throughout. I have also heard absorbing lectures on subjects so fascinating that inclusion of jocular remarks would not have improved them.

Nevertheless, everyone should know how to use funny material – perhaps in opening remarks before beginning a serious speech; or in order to soften an otherwise critical and hard-hitting statement; or to help to relax participants in a meeting, or workmates in a discussion.

In this chapter we will discuss what humour is; where you can find funny material; how to adapt it to your needs; how to write your own humour; using formulae to make it easier; how to tell your jokes well; reasons why humour fails; the importance of shared experience; useful tips for beginners.

But one warning. Don't let humour run away with you. In any speech (as opposed to a comedy routine) humour is not an end in itself but a means to an end. A string of jokes or witticisms is not a speech. The humour should be relevant to your theme and your message; it should give your speech life, not submerge it.

What Is Humour, And
What Makes People Laugh?

There are many kinds of joke. And humour has many moods. It can be aggressive, or deadpan, or sly, or warmhearted, or sick, or scoffing, or wry, or sincere, or arch. It can be gentle or insulting, intellectual or childish, witty or outrageous.

Whatever its mood, humour has to do with relationships. These relationships may involve words, ideas, things, events, people and especially the characteristics of people. They may be incongruous relationships, ironic relationships, bizarre relationships, sharply contrasting relationships.

One of the commonest kinds of joke involves deception. You lead the audience in one direction, then suddenly reveal that all the time they were being taken along a different path. When this switch of direction takes place, it is called the *punch* of the story – hence the expression, *punchline*. To be funny, you must understand this pattern: *deception,* followed by *surprise.* You lead your listeners up the garden path, then – wham, punchline!

I'm very grateful to my friends in the audience for their sympathy during my recent illness. On the night I was stricken the word flashed from person to person: Dick Smithies has dislocated his neck. And all over town that night my friends offered up the identical prayer . . . 'Dear God: Let it be Dick's vocal cords that are dislocated.'

Of course in shorter jokes, there is no time to build up deception, so the humour depends more on incongruity or wordplay or contrast: 'He's a man of many parts – very few of them in good working order.'

When the joke is longer, the deception is known as the setup, which at the last moment switches to the punchline. Rarely is the punchline funny in itself – separated from the setup, it will seem nothing more than a flat statement.

Even a one-liner may need a setup – that's the way you write it into your speech. So:

Your president, Alf Badger, is a remarkable guy – a man of fine characteristics and varied accomplishments. It can truly be said of him that he is a man of many parts . . . unfortunately he has lived such a high life that few of his parts are any longer in good working order.

The skill of moulding and massaging a joke to fit your needs can be learned – but needs practice.

Where Do You Find
Funny Material?

You don't find it, you collect it. Write down jokes that appeal to you – in a notebook, in a card index, even on scraps of paper. You will come across these especially appealing jokes when rummaging through a book of jokes, listening to TV, leafing through a magazine or chatting with friends. Immediately scribble down the gist of the joke, or at least the punchline, on any old scrap of paper. Later you can transfer these choice items to your own jokefile or jokebook – or you may just clip the scraps of paper together. The main thing is to collect funny material, think about it, rehearse it, use it, practise adapting it to your needs.

Have you ever watched one of those television comedy programmes where the panellists are asked to tell jokes on random subjects: on dogs, football, politics, religion, the weather, bachelors, bankruptcy, children – and so on? And whatever the subject the panellists *always* come up with a joke that fits. How do they do it? Have they amazing memories that file away jokes on every conceivable subject?

Of course not. What these experts do is twist a standard joke to fit the announced subject. One TV panellist may be asked to tell a joke about farmers. So she begins: 'These two farmers were in a pub . . .' and proceeds to tell a joke about two drunken farmers. The other panellists guffaw. *They* know this contestant isn't telling a joke about farmers. She's telling a joke about drunkards, which she has carefully rehearsed beforehand. Now she simply turns the joke by declaring the drunkards are farmers. If she had been asked to speak on accountancy or football, she would have trotted out the same joke: 'These two accountants were in a pub . . .' or 'These two footballers were in a pub . . .'

This technique is essential. If you have a speech to give on (say) the need to upgrade local highways, don't go rummaging through joke books hoping to find just the right joke listed under *Highways*. It won't be there. It may be listed under *Personal Insults* (that is, an insult that can be adapted to describe the person who designed the present highway system). Or it may be listed under *Women's Fashions* – a put-down of non-functional dress design which can be adapted for non-functional highway design.

This is a fundamental lesson. When looking for humorous

material, disregard the subject matter and concentrate on the point made by the joke. And when compiling your own joke file, cross reference each joke both under subject matter and under the point it makes. When you adapt a joke, you usually transfer the point of the joke to a new target. That is, you take the essential point of the joke and you re-aim it.

How To Write Your Own
Humorous Material

Everyone can write humour. It is a matter of being systematic; of knowing how to go about it; of practising. People often quit too soon. You scribble a few possible jokes, decide they are too weak, and give up. *Keep going*. Write out a dozen jokes, or twenty or thirty. Set them all down, however weak. Then tomorrow go through them again. You will find better wording for some of them; you will discover two of them can be joined; a hopelessly weak joke will suggest another that is better. Keep honing them all in the days leading up to your speech. Then choose half a dozen of the best.

Remember: you are looking for contrasts, contradictions, word-plays, incongruities, bizarre juxtapositions. For longer items you will engage in a deception, then hit your listeners with your punch-line. Choose twenty statements from your speech. Decide that each of them is a punchline: now try to work up a deception that can be twisted at the last minute to arrive at the punchline. It is the incongruity, or sheer surprise, of the punchline that triggers laughter.

Second, go through your speech looking for double meanings of words and phrases; for contrasting relationships between ideas, events, situations and people. All of these are possible sources of humour.

Third, try free association. Think about your audience: Who do they dislike and why? Who do they like and why? Who are their rivals? What are the hobbies, occupations, and unusual characteristics of well-known people among them? What recent events in the news affect them? What past events? What common sayings or slogans or advertising headlines do they relate to?

Take any of these ingredients and search for contrasts, exaggerations, odd juxtapositions, incongruities, ironies. Remember: a joke that relates to the interests of your audience will work three or four times better than one that does not.

There are dozens of formulae that make joke-writing easier. Here are just a few:

Double meanings: In a speech to lawyers, play around with double meanings of words like *court, brief, sentence, case* – and you will come up with any number of jokes. 'Any top lawyer should be able to handle three cases a week – a murder case, a divorce case . . . and a case of Scotch.'

Divergent meanings: Take well-known phrases and slide subtly into a contrasting context: 'The union keeps saying it is a grassroots movement. But from the number of strikes it has called it could better be described as a lack-of movement.'

Switch of occupation: Write down the main occupation of people in the audience, then a list of other possible occupations to see what incongruous contrasts you can come up with: 'If your doctor simply prescribes pills, rather than entering into a dialogue with you for the good of your health, then he's nothing more than a vet. And I say to you that if your doctor treats you not as if he were a doctor but as if he were a vet . . . you are entitled to bite him on the leg . . . and pee on his carpet!'

Localities: 'Levin? Isn't it the pits? Anyone who buys a ticket out of Levin isn't going on holiday – he's escaping!' Insults directed at the hometown of a noted person in your audience always go well.

Puns: 'A contraceptive is a device that should be used on every *conceivable* occasion.' Go through your speech looking for words with double meanings and shape them into jokes.

Reworked initials: 'In his wild, misspent youth, he was a member of the I.R.A. . . . the Invercargill Rhododendron Association.' Take any set of initials – preferably those of the organisation you are speaking to – and play around with them, seeking a meaning that contrasts sharply with the true nature of the organisation.

Negative-into-positive: Take something bad, dwell on its deficiencies, then enthuse over it: 'This must be one of the most obscene, nauseating, and degrading books ever written . . . I can get it for you at $20 a copy.'

Definitions: 'Sarah is the sort of person who detests exercise . . . so she has devoted her life to eating . . . and now she has the fittest set of jaws in the country.' Method: take any person, event, occupation and write down a long list of contrasting descriptions and you will come up with a definition joke.

I have space to give you only a small sampling of the dozens of formulae for writing jokes. To decide what suits you best, take ten or fifteen jokes you really like (preferably ones you have told successfully), and analyse them. By dissecting these favoured items, you will find what joke forms suit you best and in time your thought processes will begin to follow those formulae. Practise by taking a favourite joke and translating it into a different context. It is practice that counts: try to spend fifteen minutes a day at it.

How To Tell Your Joke
The Right Way

You have heard it said again and again that comedians have a special skill called timing which is denied to ordinary mortals. Another word for timing is pausation, and it is essential for joke telling.

Pausation is discussed in Chapter 6, where we look at ways of presenting a speech. It is a combination of *phrasing* (or grouping) of words; of *pausing* after a group of words; of *stressing* key words in the group; and of using *variation of voice* in the right places. The purpose of pausation, or timing, is to lodge key words with the audience and to help them combine or counterpoint different words or phrases. Pausation lets words or groups of words sink in. Whether the speech is serious or funny, pausation is the single most important aspect of good presentation.

Misuse of pausation and stress is a major reason jokes fail. Take this joke: 'The average *woman* would sooner have *beauty* than *brains* . . . because she knows the average *man* can *see* better than he can *think*.' If the stresses (in italic) and pause (the dots) are wrong, the audience will not make the connection between the setup and the punchline. If you gabble through the joke, or mumble through it, or sing-song through it, or plough through in a monotone – then the point will be lost because your listeners will not see the contrast between the key words in the setup and the key words in the punchline.

Mumbling, bred of timidity, is a particular failure. Be brave. Cruise into the joke at full throat, enunciating clearly and succinctly, letting your eyes rove over the audience, a small smile on your face; hit them with your joke, and make it stick.

And for heaven's sake look happy. Too many beginners tell jokes with strained, uncomfortable, frozen features. Relax. Don't look miserable, don't show your listeners you are worried. If you appear happy and relaxed, you will give your joke maximum chance of succeeding. Tell your joke with courage and with confidence, and if you get no response at least show by your sly smile that *you* enjoyed it.

How To Choose The Right
Target Of Your Joke

While some humour is gentle and will offend no-one, many jokes are aggressive – they have a butt, or target. That butt may be a person (the taxman), an organisation (a 'keep smut out of the movies' society), an attitude ('abortion is murder'), a belief ('psychic surgery can heal without pain or scar'), behaviour (the practice of smoking pot), or the like. Thus you are criticising either a person or something someone holds dear, and you run the risk of offending your audience, because they may sympathise with the target of the joke.

Obviously the crude insult is very risky: 'The Leader of the Opposition is a shiver looking for a spine to run up.' Or: 'Take no notice of what the Mayor says. The people of Allingham just keep him as a pet.' If your audience *likes* the target of your criticism, then the joke will not only fail but probably also upset them for the rest of your speech.

The most dangerous target of all is the audience. If you construct a joke, however funny, that homes in on the audience, you are likely to raise resentment. This is especially so if it is the first, or one of the first, jokes in your speech. Let's suppose you are addressing a group of middle-aged women to whom you say: 'After twenty years of married life the woman who once *looked* like a *siren* starts to *sound* like one.' From this audience, you will almost certainly receive (and deserve) a cool reception.

Now I don't want you to think the audience should never be the butt of your jibes. For of course they can be – and often should be. But you must prepare the way. And the best preparation is to make fun of yourself first. For just as the riskiest target of a joke is the audience, so the safest target is yourself.

Some of the world's best humorists regularly make themselves the target of much of their humour. Even better, some create serial jokes about their physical characteristics, or about alleged deficiencies in their behaviour. Ronnie Corbett regularly makes jokes about his short stature; Jack Benny made capital for years out of his supposed miserliness; Dean Martin has strung together an amazing series of jokes about what he claims is his fondness for liquor.

There is a big advantage in this formula: you end up with a really extensive collection of good material. If you are stout, specialise in jokes about obesity. I am short ('Five foot six and a half – *and don't forget the half*'), so I tell lots of jokes about my being short.

I cannot put enough stress on this point: much of the best humour has a butt or target. If you choose the wrong target your listeners will become resentful, and very likely 'turn off' for the rest of your speech. But when you make fun of yourself, the audience warms to you. More important, you smooth the way for a transition. Having first jested about yourself, you have earned the right to poke fun at others, even at the audience and at the beliefs they cherish. So keep on devising jokes about yourself. You will find after a while you will slip into a frame of mind where you constantly come up with jokes about yourself, or your occupation, or your sport or your hobbies or the topics on which you give speeches: fire safety, dress designing, industrial relations, politics, and so on.

Finally, sick jokes, cruel jokes, vengeful jokes should be taboo. The targets are too risky: your job is to maximise your chances of getting a laugh, not to minimise them!

Sexual jokes are another matter. Some of the world's finest humour revolves around sex. And also some of the world's worst. Some commonsense rules: ribald humour should never be crude, but always subtle and understated; never be the first to use a risque joke – wait to see whether other speakers resort to ribaldry and how well it is received; if a great deal hangs on the success of your speech don't take the risk; if the audience is all of the opposite sex don't take the risk, and if the audience is largely foreigners don't take the risk.

Shared Experience: The Number One Way To Get Laughs

One of the best ways of winning over any audience is to refer to some event or situation your listeners know well. So too with humour: to succeed, a joke based on shared experience will work twice as well as one that is foreign to your listeners. If a member of your club has been having difficulty growing a beard, or the manager has just given birth to twins, or another member has just been fined for a traffic offence – these are all certain subjects for good-humoured laughter when you find yourself addressing the club.

For example, you might say: 'I noticed Peter Plessingham has finally managed to cultivate a passable beard. All I can say is he looks like a door-to-door brush salesman who has swallowed his own product . . . His wife Betty says, "These days kissing Peter is like diving into a wet hedge . . .".' Most of your listeners will have ragged Peter about his new growth, so they are bound to enjoy your remarks.

Where you know the audience well (people at your place of work or in an organisation you belong to), it is easy to find shared experience to joke about. But what if you are addressing a group of strangers? Then you have to discover something you can share with them.

Experienced speakers like to arrive a little early to chat with the organisers. The conversation is never idle. They are interested in anecdotes and amusing snippets of information, about well-known people in the organisation or about some event that has everyone talking.

Perhaps you learn that the secretary Jerry Change has just wrecked his car. So you insert a little dig into your speech: 'I was not sure I'd recognise Jerry Change when I arrived, but in fact it was no trouble. He was the one wearing bicycle clips.'

Or you are told Shirley McTaggart, pride of the club, has just come fourth in the Lakeside Marathon. 'I understand Shirley McTaggart came four thousand three hundred and sixteenth in the Lakeside Marathon. . . . Which is where she would have finished if she hadn't taken that shortcut. . . . I understand she walked across the lake.'

Not only do experienced speakers try to arrive early, but they like to hear preceding speakers if they can. They are alert for any jokes or references they can tie in to their own speech. They jot down the gist of jokes that go across well. This tells them what sort of joke the audience responds to.

This point is of utmost importance: find out if you can what makes *this* gathering laugh, and revisit the scene of their merriment. It's the laugh that counts, not the originality (most humorists borrow most of their jokes). Better to get a certain laugh by re-telling the joke of a previous speaker than to bomb out with an entirely original one of your own. In fact, this is one of the safest jokes of all: the re-telling or embellishment of a piece of humour that has already gone over well.

The next step is to plant jokes among earlier speakers, if you know one of them well enough or he is prepared to play along with you. This is how it is done. The earlier speaker, Gerald Plusfours, says:

'Later this evening, ladies and gentlemen, you will hear an opposing point of view from my very good friend Dick Smithies. Take no notice of him. He doesn't know what he's talking about. He's a wee short guy . . . you'll recognise him by the tuft of hair sticking above the lectern. . . . Well no, he's not really all that short, though I did go on a car trip once when, to make room, we had to dangle Dick from the keychain . . .'

When it comes your turn you can say with mock severity: 'You've already heard from my great friend, Gerald Plusfours, who made somewhat slighting reference to me. He said I wasn't really short, but in an overfull car I could at a pinch be dangled from the keychain.' Pause, as they laugh again. 'Well now, I think any fair-minded person would say I have right of reply . . .'

Another safe way of repeating and extending a joke is to come to an arrangement with the person introducing you. Get him to make a few amusing remarks, especially ones you know you can enlarge upon. This both softens the audience so they will be more receptive to your own humour, and it gives you something to work on.

Of course, if you prearrange jokes by those who precede you, and their material falls flat, immediately abandon your intention of repeating or extending it!

Yet another way to get a nearly certain laugh is to make fun of a common enemy: the tax department, noisy neighbours, a rival baseball team. If the group of people you are talking to has just been angered by (say) a new law, then a sly dig at the politician who introduced the law will almost certainly evoke a pleased response.

I cannot stress too strongly the importance of shared experience as a way of forming a bond between speaker and audience. That's another reason, in addition to those mentioned earlier, for finding out as much as you can about your audience as part of your preparation.

Some Essential Tips
For Beginners

Even the best comedians find some of their jokes draw little or no response. Occasionally even the most accomplished comics will have a bad night or strike an unyielding audience, and will get practically no laughs. They accept such failures. It's part of being a professional humorist: they know you can't hope to hit the mirth button every time.

But for beginners it is difficult to be so unruffled. Their greatest fear is: 'If I tell a joke and it is met by ringing silence, I just know I will be crushed. I won't dare try another.'

The best way for beginners to start is to quote a relevant joke by a well-known comedian, modifying it if necessary to suit their purpose.

As Bob Hope put it . . .

Or: *I rather like the point made long ago by Groucho Marx . . .*

Or: *I think the comment that sums up this point was once made by . . .*

The audience is almost conned into laughing – who can *not* laugh at the joke of an expert? And if they don't laugh, they can hardly blame you. After all, it wasn't your joke!

Another no-risk form of humour is to use material that is both funny and full of meaning. Tell it deadpan – and if the audience do not laugh, they will not realise they were supposed to: they will think you were being serious. You will continue unperturbed, and it will be your secret that you hoped for a laugh that never came.

As a beginner, you will concentrate on one-liners. If a one-liner flops, it is easy enough to move on. But if you build up a longish story and the punchline goes splodge, the failure will be accentuated by the length of the setup.

While you are gaining experience you will concentrate in particular upon humour directed at yourself; on shared experience; and on repeating or modifying jokes used by earlier speakers. Wherever possible you will try out new jokes on your friends before using them in your speech.

As you become more adept, you will find some of your jokes go over well every time or almost every time. Treasure them. Try to use one of them as the first joke early in your speech. Don't worry that some of your audience may have heard it before – the important thing is to get that first laugh. If your first attempt fails, the audience will begin to groan inwardly. If your second effort fails also, chances are you will have 'lost' your audience and will never get them to sparkle through the rest of the evening. Indeed, when your first two or three jokes fail, it is as well to abandon most of the rest, for you may have struck the kind of unbudgeable audience that all experienced speakers encounter once in a while.

If, however, your early sure-fire jokes work well, you will find the audience is in such a good mood that even mildly funny statements are greeted with mirth thereafter.

One final tip for beginners: never use material that relies on an ethnic accent, special tricks of voice or makeup or costume. Such sophisticated work should wait until you have gained experience in easier things.

More Advanced
Use Of Humour

Beginners should not try after-dinner speeches, 'celebrity roasts' or other events where extended humour is required. But as you become more experienced you will learn to do more than just pepper your speech with occasional jokes. You will find yourself developing funny routines with punchlines piled one on top of the other. You will experiment more with your voice, and lines that would fail in the mouth of a beginner will produce satisfying bursts of laughter because of the way you present them: the pitch and inflection of your voice, expert timing, complementary gestures, use of props and so on.

Let's take this segment, from the middle of a speech to a group of 700 travel agents:

These airline people are very tidy people. When they see something sticking out of your suitcase – like a handle or wheels – they knock the flaming thing off. Then when you go back to your travel agent to complain that they smashed up your luggage, he says: 'I'm sorry, Sir, but that's an Act of God.' So now you know who God is – he's an airline baggage handler. And you all thought he was Bill Cox [head of the travel agents association] didn't you?

An inexperienced speaker might feel there is one punchline in all that – or at most two. In fact there are six – all of which worked very well before that audience of 700. To get those six bursts of laughter it is necessary to split up the segment into eight fragments – two setups and six punchlines – and to get your timing and use of voice right. In what follows S stands for setup and P stands for punchline.

S (*An arch tone*) These airline people are very tidy people. If they see something sticking out of your suitcase . . . (*pause*)
P (*Flat, deadpan tone*) . . . like a handle, or wheels . . . (*long pause*)
P (*Punchy tone*) . . . they knock the flaming thing off . . . (*pause*)
S (*Arch tone*) . . . Then when you go back to your travel agent to complain that they smashed up your luggage, he says . . . (*slight pause*)
P (*Obsequious tone*) . . . I'm sorry, Sir, but that's an Act of God . . . (*long pause*)
P (*Arch tone*) . . . So now you all know who God is . . . (*pause*)
P (*Flat, deadpan tone*) . . . he's an airline baggage handler . . . (*long pause*)
P (*Very knowing, nudge-nudge tone*) . . . And you all thought he was Bill Cox, didn't you? . . . (*very long pause*)

There are three reasons why this segment went so well: first, it relates closely to the experiences of the audience; second, the timing or pausation was right; third, the use of voice was right.

Try experimenting with timing and use of voice. Go over your joke again and again (twenty or thirty times in the course of a week if you like) lengthening the pauses, speeding up on some words, slowing down on others, altering the pitch and inflection of your voice. Try to get the feel of the words – and rewrite them again and again if necessary.

When you write multi-punchline routines, you will find it does not matter at all if some of the lines bring no response. Indeed there need to be highs and lows in the level of response. After a while, even in your ordinary speeches you will find yourself commonly using two-punchline and three-punchline jokes – not only will these increase the amount of laughter, but if you miss on one punchline the second should carry you through. Indeed, comedians commonly call the second punchline a 'saver'.

Summary

1. When borrowing jokes, look not at the subject but the point being made.

2. When writing humour, look for relationships: contrasts, exaggerations, odd juxtapositions, incongruities, ironies.

3. Choose the right target for your joke – one the audience can accept.

4. Get the pauses right and stress the key words in the setup and the punchline.

5. Jokes based on shared experience or on the experience of your audience always work best.

6. Beginners should stick to one-liners, and to the successful jokes of others.

7. With more experience you will develop two-punchline and three-punchline jokes and multiple-punchline segments.

Chapter Five

SEVEN WAYS TO IMPROVE MARKEDLY WHAT YOU WRITE AND SPEAK

Why does an occasional book flow so effortlessly and so compellingly that you do not want to be interrupted in your reading of it? Why does a rare speaker come across so hypnotically that you cannot take your eyes or ears off him?

The answer, I suggest, can be compressed into the acronym WORD-SCRIPT. In this chapter we will look at seven main elements of good use of language:

1. The WORDs you use.
2. The Sentences you form.
3. The Connectors you use to link sentences and paragraphs.
4. The Rhythm of your words and of the way you arrange them.
5. The Images formed by the words you use.
6. The Potency of the words you use.
7. The Theme that grows out of your arrangement of potent words, rhythmic sentences, artful connectors and compelling images.

There it is: WORD-SCRIPT. Remember it well.

Words: Be Thrifty
And Simple

Why do so many people insist on using unnecessary words? Are they afraid of clarity? Do they wish to obscure their meaning for fear of being challenged? Or do they delight in wordiness out of sheer pomposity? Maybe none of these: I suspect they do not think clearly, and it comes through in what they say. The converse is surely true: that if you take pains to express yourself precisely, you will begin to think more precisely.

One sin is the gushing adjective: *awfully, terribly, frightfully, amaz-*

ingly, horribly, very. Leave it out altogether, or substitute a less over-worked word. Beware too the unnecessary qualifier:

– I was *quite* interested in his new book.
– It's *rather* fun to be Girl Friday in an all-male crew.
– I *really* don't know why politicians have to be so devious.

In each case the italicised word nervously waters down a simple statement, and makes it less clear.

At the opposite extreme are those redundant words that add emphasis where none is needed: an *unfilled* vacancy; a *grave* emergency; a *wild* rumour; his *particular* job; three *possible* ways of doing it; *in the field of* continuing education; the *end* result.

In each case the italicised word or words should be omitted. A common redundancy is *at this point in time,* which means *now.* But I have heard it worse: *at this particular point in time.* And worse still: *at this particular point in time of history!*

As a general rule, be sparing of adjectives: concentrate on using nouns and verbs. This will help you avoid redundancies.

Another cause of wordiness is use of awkward phrases where one word would be better:

owing to the fact that – since
are in a position to – can
points up the fact that – shows
the question as to whether – whether
always provided that – if
in the vicinity of – near
with the exception of – except
which means that – so
is capable of – can
he is a man who – he

There are dozens, probably hundreds, of such clumsy expressions in common use. Identify them, and expunge them from your working vocabulary.

Then of course there are those single words that are longer and less satisfying than their briefer alternatives:

supplementary – extra
inception – beginning
subsequently – later
currently – now
approximately – about
provided – if

deceased – dead
ascertain – discover
predominantly – mainly
residence – home

Why would anyone use *donor and donee* when *giver and receiver* is available? Why talk of *domestic friction* when you mean *family arguments?* Why say people are *domiciled at* when they *live at?*

People who do not have a passion for words, who do not consult dictionaries regularly, who do not revise and rehearse what they write and say, can hardly expect to express themselves clearly. Good use of language has never come easily to anyone, and needs to be worked at if there is to be no slipping back. (Everyone has lapses, and I am sure I have had some in writing this book.)

Anyone who works in a complex discipline is exposed to the jargon of his or her calling: academics, scientists, lawyers, doctors, bureaucrats, politicians, economists and the like. When speaking to a lay audience they must, and when speaking to their equals they should, render the jargon in simple terms.

I have had this out many times with lawyers who want 'legal precision' in speeches of a legal nature, but shamelessly demand simplicity in scientific speeches; conversely scientists have wanted 'scientific precision' in scientific speeches but simplicity in legal speeches! As a lifelong editor I have seen this partisanship among economists, engineers, doctors, scientists – always they want their own jargon but they would prefer that the other person should not confuse them with his! I can only say that in twenty-five years of writing and editing I have yet to discover a technical expression that could not be rendered in words understandable to the lay person.

Sentences: Keep Them
Short, Crisp, Direct

We have seen that, wherever possible, words and phrases should be short and simple. Much the same applies to sentences.

When speaking you will find often that you break the conventional rules of sentence structure: 'What did he do then? Bunged it straight through the window. Crazy. Didn't prove a thing. As the cop tried to tell him.' An expert speaker will split up these groups of words with pauses of varying length. His voice will lift, subside, halt, leap into motion again. For him, grammar is pausation, inflec-

tion of voice, a roller-coaster rise and fall in the delivery of his
words.

Beware long sentences. Worst of all are those containing wander-
ing phrases and meandering subordinate clauses. Audiences easily
become confused when you combine several ideas in a single
sentence. Best of all is a mixture of short and medium sentences,
with an occasional long one.

Your sentences should most often be in the active voice, rather
than the passive. In other words, they should be direct statements,
rather than being turned upside down into indirect statements. In
the following examples, (a) is passive and (b) is active:

(a) *The regulations were rammed through by sheer force of will.*
(b) *By sheer force of will, the secretary rammed the regulations through.*

(a) *It is doubtful the marathon could be won by Mary.*
(b) *Mary has little chance of winning the marathon.*

(a) *There were a great number of obstacles to be overcome.*
(b) *He faced many daunting obstacles.*

Wherever possible, express your sentences in positive rather than
negative form. In the following examples, (a) is negative and (b) is
positive.

(a) *He did not like going to church.*
(b) *He disliked going to church.*

(a) *The result did not seem to help much.*
(b) *The result was unhelpful.*

(a) *She did not pay any attention to her boss's advice.*
(b) *She ignored what her boss said.*

Vigorous speech depends much upon economy of words and
directness of expression. When your sentences are woolly, usually
you have let words get in each other's way; or have cobbled them
together in unhappy fashion; or have used several words where one
would be more vivid.

Take special care, in the way you construct your sentences, to
avoid ambiguity: 'Alfred Quibble couldn't come, and the committee meeting was a great success.' To remove the ambiguity,
replace *and* either with *and this meant* or with *but nevertheless*.

Connectors: Use Them To Link
Sentences and Paragraphs

When speaking or writing, you should group your sentences in 'paragraphs'. A paragraph may be a single sentence, but more commonly is three, four or five sentences. Sometimes more. Written paragraphs are indicated by indentation, or a space; in speech, paragraphs are separated by pauses.

The purpose of paragraphs is to gather together statements that form a single idea, or that form a separate step in your unfolding account. But it is not enough just to plop down a group of four or five sentences, pause, then plop down another group. That produces a disjointed, episodic effect your audience will find hard to follow. You must connect your paragraphs – and you must also link the sentences within your paragraphs.

Connectors are words and phrases that help carry your story forward. They link up your ideas; meld your evidence into your line of argument; give flow to your discourse. To be skilful in making these transitions is one of the finer arts of writing and speaking. To use vivid connectors with a flair for logic, sequence and balance is the essence of good style.

Some connectors reach back to a previous sentence or paragraph and hook it firmly into the present sentence or paragraph. Each of the following statements, coming at the beginning of a paragraph, links it with the preceding paragraph, and at the same time carries the idea forward:

– *This would clearly take some time.*
– *Now why does that always happen?*
– *That was his undoing.*
– *I say: don't believe her.*
– *Without this assurance, the government could hardly budge.*
– *Not so: his placid nature is well known to everyone.*
– *That's what I'd been trying to tell her.*

Note how pronouns (*this, that, his, her*) are used as a bridge in many of these transitional sentences.

While some connectors reach back, others push ahead to plant hooks in future sentences and lock them into what has already been said:

– *Now you will see where I am heading.*

- *This brings me to the real issue.*
- *Let us see what alternatives might be tried.*
- *Here I must jump forward several years.*
- *I want now to refer to a quite different controversy.*

Most people use connectors in groping fashion, and often it is pretty much luck when they hit upon a link-word (or -phrase or -sentence) that ties parts of their discourse together satisfactorily.

If you understand the different forms these linkages may take, and their infinite variety, you will become increasingly skilled at achieving a smooth, flowing transition from one thought to the next.

Most simple connectors are single words and they can be grouped according to the relationship they establish between two ideas. They may carry your story forward in several ways:

1. By adding new points — *and, also, indeed, moreover, another, in addition, next, then, another point, besides.*

2. By establishing a relationship of similarity — *likewise, similarly, in the same way.*

3. By qualifying or counterpointing what has just been said — *nevertheless, however, but, and yet, still, despite this, unfortunately, even so, conversely, on the contrary.*

4. By posing a question — *Now why did he do that? Can anyone believe such a story?*

5. By presenting an alternative — *Of course X should also be considered. Either we can do A or we can do B. Not only was he Y but also Z.*

6. By establishing cause and effect — *as a result, so, thus, in other words, because, consequently, therefore, hence, and that is why, it follows, accordingly.*

7. By establishing a relationship in time — *presently, the next day, meanwhile, soon, next, while, then, before, previously, all afternoon.*

8. By establishing a relationship in space — *across the street, on the next farm, whenever he came to a cross-roads, beyond this point, right next to the bakery.*

9. By giving examples — *to illustrate, likewise, for instance, in particular, for example.*

10. By using repetition for emphasis – *indeed, in other words, namely, in reality, that is to say, in fact.*

Many connectors (*moreover, and, therefore, in fact, on the other hand*) become weakened by familiarity. There is nothing wrong with them if used sparingly, but don't become attached to them. Instead, try to make your transitions vivid and eloquent, especially where they link paragraphs:

- *That last remark is bound to get me into trouble.*
- *So remember the moral in all this.*
- *My, what a blunder that turned out to be.*
- *To have done so without warning would have been unforgivable.*
- *Why ever not, any sane person might ask.*
- *They were soon to discover how rapidly their friends would forsake them.*
- *'Bloody liar,' was his boss's response.*

Soon you will find that no longer are you plopping down sentences and paragraphs that don't hang together. With practice you will begin to think in terms of smooth transitions that fold one step of your story into the next:

How could anyone have guessed that only three days after inheriting such riches she would put a gun in her mouth and splatter the top of her head across the bathroom ceiling . . . That's what I want to talk about tonight: why this tormented young woman threw away, even before she had begun to experience it, the kind of lifestyle millions of us can only dream about.

This paragraph both locks into the preceding one and reaches out to those that will follow.

Work upon your connectors. They are the bridges that tie your ideas together, giving your listeners the clear impression that you know where you are going. They are the essence of good development. Of course, they should not be overdone. Your sentences should be a mixture of two kinds: those that make linkages backward and forward to tie your story together; and those that simply push the story forward.

Rhythm: Put Flow
Into Your Phrasing

Both speakers and writers must have an ear for words. Especially speakers. How you arrange your words and phrases will determine the extent to which you can achieve rise and fall in your utterances. Jam several words of multi syllables together, and your statement will be jerky. Be too sparse with adjectives and you may need to insert one simply to make a sentence flow well. Sometimes you will repeat a word or phrase not merely for emphasis but to achieve the right lilt and cadence. Often, when preparing a speech, you will rearrange the words and phrases of a sentence several times until you are satisfied with the ring of it as you speak it out loud.

Unlike poets, speakers do not have to be regular in their rhythms, nor is it desirable, for they would quickly become singsong. When a poet begins in iambic rhythm (groups of two syllables, the first unstressed the second stressed), he will normally continue in that rhythm. Not so the speaker, who will readily switch from soft-heavy stress (iambic) to heavy-soft (trochaic) to soft-soft-heavy (anapestic) to heavy-soft-soft (dactylic).

More important, a speaker may run lightly through a group of words, playing down the differences in stress – then *wham,* hit every important syllable in his next group of words with uncommon emphasis. He or she may also omit words, presenting ungrammatical portions of sentences, if that helps the statements to flow more vividly. For a speaker, phrases are paramount.

When a speaker's tongue trips often on what he or she asks it to say, usually the fault is bad phrasing and rhythm: 'This multipresentational advertising technique inhibits effectiveness whereas a single-presentational format promotes maximum levels of sales.' What a jumble. Who could say that lot eloquently? But try rewording it: 'If you use a shotgun method in your advertising, trying to reach every prospect with one mammoth blast, you will hit no-one. But if you identify your quarry, drop him with a single rifle-shot, then turn your gun patiently on other selected targets, in the end your total kill will be far larger for the same expenditure of ammunition.' Not only are the words and phrases more vivid now, but they can be said with compelling voice rhythms.

Whether you want to speak or write, work on rhythm until it becomes engrained in you. Sometimes, of course, you will be defeated by the bad rhythms of others: when you wish to quote an eminent person from a book or newspaper. If the words you want to use are unspeakable, you may need to paraphrase some of them – perhaps ending with only one sentence that is a direct quotation.

Imagery: Paint
Pictures With Words

At a conference, any experienced speaker dislikes being brought on directly after lunch. Below her, the participants are settling into comfortable chairs, clasping their hands across over-full stomachs. With foreboding, she realises half her audience is likely to doze off and the rest will be only vaguely attentive.

Yet it need not be so. If you hit your listeners where they think, then hit them again, and again, you will jolt them alert. Having grasped each by the brain, you should be able to retain their attention throughout your session. How?

1. Use concrete words and phrases, not abstract ones.
2. Avoid statistics, figures and other sleep-inducers.
3. Use words so they build pictures as beguiling as those in any comic book or TV programme.
4. Use imagery – especially metaphor and simile – to bring your message alive.
5. Insert your listeners into the picture you sketch, by using the magic words *you, your* and *we*.

All the most compelling writers and speakers follow this rule: 'Show them, don't tell them.' Try to avoid such generalised, abstract statements as: 'Inflation has increased prices by an average of 5 per cent for the last forty years.' Be concrete and specific, as in the example given on page 24, in which the march of inflation is depicted through the changing price and character of a meat pie.

Use concrete words that evoke pictures. In the following pairs, the first sentence is abstract, the second concrete:

(a) *His dislike of politicians was intense and unwavering.*
(b) *Whenever given the chance, he would bellow to the world: 'In my opinion, all politicians fall somewhere below orang-outangs on the social scale.'*

(a) *When social injustice becomes intolerable, people are entitled to use violence against their oppressors.*
(b) *When the Nazis trucked innocent Jews by the thousands to the ovens of Auschwitz and Treblinka, they proved for all time that persecution can become so monstrous that people are entitled to revolt against and destroy their oppressors.*

Very often, turgid expressions involve figures and statistics: 'The latest surveys show 63.2 per cent of the population agree with Barclay's position, and only 28.9 per cent agree with Hamilton's position, with 7.9 per cent undecided.' Now how could any listener take that in, sort it out, and be ready for your next statement? How much clearer, how much more vivid it is, to say: 'For every person who sided with Hamilton on this issue, two lined up behind Barclay.'

Wherever possible, turn percentages into images; failing that into fractions ('in the last ten years thefts increased by one half and rapes by one third'); and where you are really stuck, round them off ('a little more than 70 per cent today against less than 40 per cent twelve years ago').

Similarly, turn measurements into pictures. Nobody can visualise a hole thirty-five metres deep, so translate it into an image:

By mid-morning the underground water had done its mischief. Quite suddenly the back lawn of the vicarage slumped. Within an hour the unseen forces had opened a massive hole deep enough to have taken four houses piled one upon the other. At the bottom of that hole the broken vicarage sat alone.

Forget the thirty-five metres. Give them a hole they can imagine.

If you really try you can paint a landscape full of measurements without using a numeral:

Sally lived on a small farm no wider than a city block and only thrice as long. It was bounded on three sides by gorse hedges stout enough to deter her rambunctious Galloway bull, and on the fourth by a weed-choked stream so narrow that in places Sally could jump it with ease. Her house was no more than a cottage, set at one end of the property under a pimple-like hill, upon which she had planted pine trees to increase the protection it gave from the prevailing northerly.

Get people into your account if you can, but don't refer to them in the abstract: 'One person has bitterly criticised the town council's failure to maintain the road.' *One person?* Who? And what's he like?

Give the people in your story names and descriptions, mannerisms and voices; make them do things, reveal their emotions, come into conflict with others:

Jim Blount is a big red-headed, red-faced Irishman with a voice roughened by making itself understood to distant sheepdogs. He lives at the very end of

Corrugation Road; that road rules his life, and it is by that road that his farm thrives or fails. For years, Jim Blount made known he would set his best dog upon the Chairman of the Council if Corrugation Road were not mended. For years, nothing happened. So last week Jim Blount loaded his tip-truck high with near-liquid manure and bounced his way towards town. All along the route he made his intention plain, leaning repeatedly from the window of his cab to roar, 'Which way to the town hall?' Whereupon with a grimace halfway to madness, he would clutch the wheel anew, urging his reeking vehicle onward, giving no sign he had noticed his neighbours dashing inside to the phone.

That's right, Jim Blount is that same man. He's that 'person who has bitterly criticised the town Council's failure to maintain the road'. But no longer is he skulking behind vague abstract words; by use of specifics, he has come alive. And at the same time his problem road has become real to your listeners.

That's picture-making with words. Then there are figures of speech, such as similes and metaphors. Let's suppose you are speaking about the world's down-trodden peoples. Don't say: 'We have all got to be aware of the tragedy of violent death in far-off lands.' Hit your audience with a metaphor: 'Go out of your house in the early morning just before dawn, and turn your face to the hills. Very soon you will see the sun peep over those ramparts . . . sloshing the world's blood up your sky. There's no escaping it. As the planet turns, those swatches of crimson are thrust before the eyes of nation after nation. Yet who really sees them, who really comprehends . . .?'

Teach yourself to think constantly in comparisons, especially metaphor and simile. These figures of speech employ the magic of analogy and resemblance: they illuminate our understanding by using images to heighten meaning. As we shall see soon, many clichés once were vivid metaphors and similes; through constant repetition they have lost their freshness and potency. But worn figures of speech can be revived if you transfer the comparison to another context, as the following pairs show:

(a) *It was like trying to find a needle in a haystack.*
(b) *It was like casting a net into the Atlantic at random, in hope of snaring a fish that may not even exist.*

(a) *She found she had been left holding the baby.*

67

(b) *To her dismay, the glittering prize she had so coveted now splintered into embarrassing pieces in her hands – while her colleagues stared impassively and unhelpfully from a distance.*

(a) *One glance told me poor old Alf was at death's door.*
(b) *One glance at poor old Alf told me the undertaker could begin calculating his fee.*

Make metaphor your friend and your preoccupation. All of us know someone who is such an habitual blunderer that he worsens every difficult situation he encounters. How should we describe such a person so that the description grips our listeners? Try this lovely metaphor: 'He's the sort of person who just can't help throwing petrol on fires.'

Ah yes, let good use of imagery be your obsession.

Potent Words: Make
Them A Habit

We saw earlier how redundant words and clumsy expressions can fudge and obscure your meaning. Equally destructive are clichés, those threadbare phrases so debased from repetition that they have lost all sharpness and freshness. I have in my files a list of 700 of these hand-me-down expressions, and there must be several thousand in common use. Indeed, in 1940 Eric Partridge published a *Dictionary of Clichés* that filled 250 pages.

Clichés are phrases that once were alive and kicking, but which now are the be-all and end-all of the lazy speaker who does not know how to call a spade a spade. Instead, he bores us to death with his common or garden platitudes, and as a general rule of thumb you could say he is forever at sixes and sevens, chewing more than he has bitten off, and constantly beating about the bush.

When he gets his second wind he sets off again like a giant refreshed, going from strength to strength; but his utterances fail miserably to hit the nail on the head as he leaves no stone unturned in his efforts to shed light on the subject. Though he is not on good speaking terms with the language, the right word is always on the tip of his tongue. You can be sure he is in deadly earnest even if he is far from accurate, and his words most emphatically do not carry a wealth of meaning.

The cliché-user knows the ropes. He can lay it on with a trowel if left to his own devices. He doesn't need a helping hand to lick any piece of prose into shape. He won't mince matters. Without a shadow of a doubt he will sit on the fence, with his ear to the ground and his best foot forward, ruling the roost as he rolls up his sleeves, puts his shoulder to the wheel andl works his fingers to the bone. Just when you think he is skating on the thin end of the wedge, he will take the wind out of your sails by asking you a very vexed question like a bolt from the blue. In an agony of uncertainty you will wrestle with your conscience, unable to make head nor tail of his bone of contention. Finally when at your wits' end you will beat a hasty retreat, duck off the beaten track, reach the end of your tether, turn with your back to the wall, take off your boot and put it on the other foot, collapse in a bundle of nerves, and beg him to bury the hatchet.

The cliché-user is a blot on the landscape. Constantly he condemns himself out of his own mouth. He subjects language to a fate worse than death. Regrettably he is never conspicuous by his absence, but rather the opposite is the case. If there was any justice, the cliché-user would be seen and not heard. His lips would be sealed, and in that way the punishment would truly fit the crime.

The preceding four paragraphs are composed almost entirely of clichés. I count sixty-three of them. If you get more than that, I've included some I did not recognise!

Some clichés are so dreadful they carry an in-built groan: *from the bottom of my heart; it made my blood boil; a voice crying in the wilderness; the burning question; as thick as thieves; stick to his guns.*

But others are more seductive: *in good hands; a forlorn hope; curiously enough; in less than no time; I can safely say; bright and early.*

Clichés are most destructive when they are connectors, for they weaken those essential bridges between ideas: *At long last; The inevitable conclusion; As a matter of fact; All things considered; Again and again.*

How do you achieve freshness and potency in the words you use? Go out and buy a good dictionary of synonyms and antonyms. (I like *The Nuttall Dictionary of English Synonyms and Antonyms*, London/ New York, 1980, and *The Doubleday Roget's Thesaurus in Dictionary Form*, New York, 1977.) Then try to wear it out.

Instead of saying someone was *brassed off*, choose from: *annoyed, vexed, piqued, affronted, nettled, irritated.*

Rather than use the cliché *black-hearted*, try *wicked, depraved, villainous, malevolent, base, corrupt, vile, evil.*

There's no need to use such a tired expression as *ruled the roost* when you have the choice of: *autocratic, imperious, arrogant, arbitrary, domineering, dictatorial, overweening.*

Immerse yourself in synonyms, and you will more easily find the right word. That is not merely the word closest to the shade of meaning you want, but (for the speaker) the one that fits best into the rhythm of the phrase in which he will use it. Above all, speakers should try to use onomatopoeic words. That is, words formed from sounds that suggest the object or action they describe. Consider swish, or flinch, or slither, or lash. How you can curl your lips and your tongue around such words. Try thwack, or splatter. Then there's sizzle, crackle, swoon, clutter, slosh, cringe, slash, slobber. In each case, the sound reinforces the meaning, and you as a speaker must bring out that sound.

Theme: Let Everything Advance It

The Russian writer Anton Chekhov once emphasised the importance of relevance thus: 'If at the beginning of your story you mention a gun hanging on the wall, then sooner or later in your story that gun must be fired.'

That's an exaggeration, and intentionally so. But it makes the point: everything you say or write should advance your purpose. Build your account inexorably, with evidence and argument that pushes your story forward. Weed out irrelevancies. Shun purple prose that uses words for their own sake rather than for the development of your theme.

In this chapter we have looked at seven ways in which you can improve your use of language. Seven techniques involving WORDs, Sentences, Connectors, Rhythm, Imagery, Potency and Theme. WORD-SCRIPT. But that's only a start. There are hundreds of lessons to be learned about good and bad use of language whether written or spoken. Try that superb little book *The Elements of Style,* by William Strunk and E. B. White (New York/London, 1979). That will bother you, for it identifies common errors all of us make. And it will spur you to read more widely, to experiment, to rehearse your utterances, and revise your writings.

Summary

1. Choose short, simple words; avoid clumsy expressions; be sparing with adjectives.

2. Keep your sentences short, crisp, direct; use the active voice not the passive; use positive rather than negative expressions; avoid ambiguity.

3. Use vivid connectors that carry your story forward by locking your present statement back to what you have already said, or hooking it into something you will soon say.

4. Flowing rhythm in your phrasing will help people to understand and will give richness to your meaning.

5. Use vivid imagery; paint pictures with words; make metaphor and simile your preoccupation.

6. Choose potent words; avoid clichés or revitalise them; spend time on synonyms and antonyms.

7. To build your theme, ruthlessly excise every word, phrase, sentence and paragraph that does not advance your purpose.

Chapter Six

WHY EXPERIENCED SPEAKERS
COME ACROSS SO WELL

When an experienced speaker strides to the platform, she takes control. For the next half hour, or an hour, she will hold the audience in thrall. She will inform them, amaze them, inspire them, amuse them, play delicate tunes upon their emotions. And they will all feel secure, enjoying the fact that she is in command.

Preparing a speech is only half the effort. Equally important is the way it is presented. Good presentation can so enliven a bad speech as to make it memorable. Conversely, bad presentation can ruin a brilliantly constructed speech.

Bad presentation is of two kinds:

1. *The speaker fails to take charge.* She is timid, quiet, stumbling, apologetic, dull.

2. *The speaker takes charge in the wrong way.* She is over-forceful, putting forward her opinions in an aggressive, patronising way. She lectures, she rants, she preaches, she hectors, she shouts.

Your aim must always be to control your audience, in the nicest possible way. To show them you are in control, that they are secure in your hands. To demonstrate sincerity, good humour, sensitivity to their feelings. To persuade them, and in so doing to enrich their experience.

In this chapter we will discuss the skills of good presentation: how to use voice, gesture, eye contact, pausation, facial expression, pace, volume, enunciation and good breathing to enhance and enlarge what you have to say. Many of these skills will assist you in everyday life, in your job and on social occasions. We will be discussing not only how you present your speech but in a sense how you present yourself.

Avoid Reading Your Speech
If At All Possible

My advice on reading a speech is: don't. If at all possible, avoid having a prepared script. That makes you a reader, not a speaker, and you may as well be replaced by a tape recorder.

On some occasions you will have to follow a script: if you are delivering a complex scientific paper to a conference; if you are setting out a legally binding arrangement; if you are presenting a politically sensitive decision or any other statement which must be adhered to word for word. There is still much you can do to liven your presentation.

Place the typed pages on the lectern – then walk away. Stand before the audience and begin as you would if you were scriptless. Establish eye contact, ask a question, tell a joke or recount an anecdote:

'Hands up all those in the audience who are lawyers?' Seven hands go up.

'I always ask that question to see whether I'm outnumbered.' There is a mild stirring of amusement.

'Tonight I see I am not.' A burst of laughter follows.

So, without touching your script, you have established rapport with your audience.

Next, having learned it by heart, you deliver the first paragraph while still standing before the audience.

Then, and only then, do you step back to the lectern and begin reading your speech. The typescript will have wide margins wherein, every few paragraphs, you will have entered instructions in red. Those red notes in the margin indicate that you will look up from the script to deliver an anecdote or aside or joke or embellishment. Again you can step away from the lectern to do so. In this way you will interrupt the reading process and re-establish rapport with the audience. One of the best methods of breaking the reading of a script is to point to a chart or diagram propped on an easel; or to write on the blackboard; or to display an interesting object; or to screen a picture with a slide or overhead projector.

So, if you have to use a script, depart from it as often as you can. Remember, when reading, to use the same techniques as if you were speaking without a text – rise and fall of voice, pausation, enunciation, and so on.

Better than a full script is a set of notes. These should be written clearly on small cards, about 13 × 8 cm, which will fit in the palm of your hand when held vertically. (Don't try to hide them.) On these will be written 'trigger words' to guide you through your speech. With a little practice you will find that you can speak easily from such cards. Don't make your notes any bigger or they will be distracting, and they may then contain so much material that you will begin reading from them.

Never look down at your notes. Hold them cupped in your palm about chest level, and when you want to refer to them, raise them a little to almost eye level, flicking a sideways glance to catch the trigger words. In this way, with a little practice, you will find you can use note-cards as a prompt without ever losing eye-contact with the audience.

Quite the best way of presenting your speech is without any notes at all. Indeed, when giving a social speech it is not good form to use notes – your comments should seem spontaneous. And for many other speeches, especially short ones, it greatly enhances the effect to speak without prompt cards.

Throughout this book I assume you will be speaking without notes or with prompt cards only.

How To Use Gesture To Liven Your Performance

Many speakers have trouble knowing what to do with their hands. Some dangle them ape-like at their sides; others clasp them behind their backs in imitation of Prince Philip; some hold them in front as if to hide sudden nakedness; others stuff them in their pockets and even jingle coins. Some scratch their ears, pull their noses, rub the back of their necks, brush back their hair, remove their spectacles – all to cover the awkwardness of those hands.

Your hands are part of your on-stage personality. Use them well, and you will improve the presentation of your speech. Use them badly, and you will seem stiff and stilted.

Most speakers realise they should use gesture, but frequently they do it badly. It is frustrating to try and liven your presentation with expressive hand movements, only to find you have made matters worse. But don't give up. Here's a simple answer to the problem: *most bad gestures are cramped and chopping because they are done from the wrist or elbow, instead of from the shoulder.*

When listening to other speakers, watch their hand movements closely. Then practise before a mirror. First, stand the wrong way.

Clasp your hands in front of you, fig-leaf fashion, with head slightly bowed, and see how narrow your shoulders have become, how cringing and nervous your appearance. Then stand erect, shoulders back, arms ready to move in fulsome sweeps. Already you will notice how much more confident you look.

Now gesture the wrong way. Move your *lower* arms outward from the elbow, first the left and then the right, saying as you do: 'On the one hand the unions want more money, but on the other hand they want shorter hours.' The gestures are appropriate ('on the one hand . . . on the other') but note that your *upper* arms, above the elbow, move only slightly and the whole effect is cramped and ineffectual.

Now try again, still facing the mirror. This time let your left hand sweep out in a long flowing movement that involves the whole arm.

You will notice immediately what a difference it makes to move freely from the shoulder. You will notice too, that your head moves and maybe your hips, even your feet. And of course arm gestures can go not only from side to side but forward and back. Thus if you thrust a probing right forefinger at the audience your right shoulder will move forward and the entire line of your body will change.

You will see that gesture can involve the whole of your body, including change in your facial expression. This is the real secret of good use of gesture. It's not done with hands alone, but with the whole body. Don't try to move your arms alone. Your head will also move; your hips may swivel slightly; one foot may slip a little forward; and your facial expression may change.

All of this must become second nature, like driving a car. An experienced driver doesn't say to herself, 'Let in the clutch, ease your foot off the accelerator, move the gear lever, release the clutch, depress the accelerator, start turning the steering wheel . . .' She does all of that automatically – though when learning to drive she *did* have to recite each step to herself.

So too with speaking. Initially a speaker has to concentrate on the individual movements. But after a while they become automatic. At one and the same time you can: grin wickedly; toss an imaginary document to the ground; make a grinding motion with your foot; and declare with a slight flick of your head: 'And the Mayor thought he would get away with *that*!'

'Is It All Right
To Wander About?'

I have spoken first of gesture because I don't want you to get fixed ideas about the way you should stand – and then find this cramps your use of gesture.

Try to avoid any physical barrier between you and the audience. Come out from behind the table. Avoid using a lectern if you can, and shun the microphone wherever possible. Each of these – table, lectern, microphone – is a barrier between you and the audience. Microphones are worst because they tie your head to a spot a few inches from the mike and prevent normal relaxed movement of head and body.

Never lean on the table. It looks bad, it prevents gesture, and it ruins audience contact. Never lean on anything else. I once watched in amazement as a speaker pulled his chair from behind the table, placed it in front of him, put both of his hands on its back and rocked it gently back and forth, staring at the floor through the whole of his address. I have also seen a speaker lean against the wall, arms folded, staring at a window on the opposite side of the room.

If you are a beginner, never pace up and down. It distracts the audience, and prevents you from establishing eye-contact with them. While experienced speakers may sometimes manage to wander about without damaging effect, beginners are best advised to stand squarely in front of the audience with weight firmly on both feet. Your feet should move very little throughout, only one or two steps at a time. Don't hop from foot to foot (some speakers do the most remarkable little jigs) and don't slouch on one hip, then the other. Avoid a slumped posture, at one extreme; and stiff neck and ramrod back at the other extreme. Stand naturally, facing forward, because that is the best way of maintaining eye contact with the audience.

Eye Contact and
Facial Expression

Eye contact is one of the most potent skills a speaker has. It is crucial in establishing rapport with the audience. Many speakers recall with wonderment and awe the first time they experienced the feeling of 'holding' the audience. As your eyes rove over the people in front of you, you suddenly realise that every one of them is gazing at you, and hanging on your next word.

You may be a little puzzled at this point. If there are 200 people in the audience, how can you look at all of them? Easy: while you are speaking, let your eyes flow along the front few rows, left to right; then the next few rows, right to left; and so on to the back of the hall. Then work from the back rows to the front again. With experience, eye contact comes naturally. Every person in the audience will then have the feeling that you are speaking directly to him or her. None will feel left out (as they will if you concentrate on a knot of people directly in front of you). I can't stress too strongly the importance of eye contact in establishing rapport with an audience. Yet so many speakers turn side-on, with the inevitable result that only a small wedge of the audience is contacted and soon those people become uncomfortable because the contact is too intense. Meanwhile, the rest of the audience feels ignored.

The close partner of eye contact is facial expression. Frozen or twisted features, angry expression, tightly drawn lips, unsmiling eyes can all alienate an audience. Many speakers, when they become worked up, unknowingly adopt alarming expressions. It is much better if you can smile. Use a friendly smile, a tolerant smile, an exasperated smile, a wicked smile, a grim smile – but a *smile*.

Where you want to express anger (say at the brutal killing of a child), try to let your words rather than your expression indicate your disgust. Of course, you will use ringing tones to make plain your abhorrence, but let the words express your loathing, not the fury of your features.

This leads me into the perils of vehemence, of over-emphatic speaking.

Let Your Choice Of Words
Take The Place Of Vehemence.

As we saw earlier, some speakers take charge in the wrong way. There are two traps: the first is to preach to your listeners, the second, and worse, is to bully them. Both spring from the same fault: the speaker is not sensitive to the audience. It is easy to become so rapt in your own thoughts that you punch out your message in an over-emphatic, domineering manner. Remember: your task is to persuade your listeners, not to ram your views down their throats.

As speaker, you are in command, so the audience is helpless if you slip into a hectoring, declamatory delivery. Your listeners will quickly become uncomfortable. 'This speaker is preaching to me,' they will think. Worse, you may introduce such vehemence, such fury and violence into your voice that they will think you are bullying them – and, with good reason. Many bad speakers shout. Some of them harangue their listeners unforgivably. They have no prospect of persuading anyone to their point of view. They come across as truculent, opinionated and intolerant.

How much better it is to choose words so charged with meaning that they will grab the audience without being shouted. If you seem to be losing the attention of your listeners, don't raise your voice – *lower* it. People will then strain to hear. At the same time, use words that grip their emotions, and you will have their attention more surely than if you shout and harangue.

Let your words, rather than sheer volume, express your disgust: 'They are out for blood. But they are not tigers. They are hyenas, slavering over a secondhand carcase.' If it is scorn you want to project, say quietly: 'They have asked him to carry an armful of eggs over broken ground, just so they could joggle his elbow at every step.'

Often in this book I stress the importance of displaying conviction and sincerity. Vehemence is the worst enemy of sincerity. Remember this: if you speak constantly in a loud hectoring tone, you will have nowhere to go (except to shout even louder) when you want to stress something. The effect is quite dreadful. Emphasis can be achieved in many ways: by pausation; by repetition; by suddenly lowering the voice; by *smoothly* raising the voice after having lowered it; and by dramatic choice of words.

One reason for shouting is that the speaker enunciates badly: words are unclear, slurred, run together. Knowing subconsciously that his words are unclear, he shouts to try to be better understood.

If you use vehemence, make it brief (if you emphasise everything you emphasise nothing). And do watch your facial expression. Keep light and shade in your voice. Raise it, then lower it. Smile, even if it is a sarcastic smile. Don't allow yourself to adopt a stony, hard-eyed expression.

Ability To Hold A Silence
Demonstrates Mastery

Novices are afraid of pause. And they are terrified of silence. Some gabble frantically to prevent the least hesitation in their speech. Indeed, many talented speakers are ruined by breakneck delivery.

Pausation is one of the most effective tools a speaker can use. Pauses in the right places allow significant statements time to sink in; they give the audience space to applaud or to laugh; they separate ideas that otherwise could become jumbled; they help develop the structure of the speech.

Pauses can come at the end of a 'paragraph' or group of sentences; at the end of a sentence; in the middle of a sentence; several times within a sentence; or even after every word in a sentence.

Pauses can last one second; or four or five seconds. Or they can be long ringing silences of eight or ten seconds.

Now how could *anyone* hold a silence that long? By making it seem natural and by ensuring something is happening during the silence.

Let's suppose you have outlined the failings of an important public figure, your voice rising as you declaim: 'He is the Great Over-reactor. He deals with every little difficulty by mounting a full Charge of the Light Brigade.'

Then stop. The audience will for some seconds be caught up in the imagery of this public figure leading futile horseback charges to devastating defeat. Meanwhile your eyes rove over the audience. You smile. As the seconds multiply, that eye contact and that wicked smile will bridge the silence until your next words carry the speech forward.

Pauses always seem much longer to the speaker than to the audience. This is because he cannot see himself. For the audience, the change of the speaker's expression, how he moves his head and body, are events that help fill in the gap. To prove this to yourself, record a speech both on a tape recorder and on a video recorder. When the voice tape is played back, some silences will seem quite long; but when the video tape is screened those silences will probably disappear.

Silences become awkward when it is obvious they are unintentional. The speaker stops at an inappropriate point, maybe in mid-sentence, his face shows concern, he fumbles with his notes. It

79

is obvious something has gone wrong.

Awkward silences usually occur when the speaker loses concentration and becomes too self-aware. Instead of focussing on what he should be saying, instead of *giving out* to his listeners, he becomes too conscious of the audience *pressing in* upon him – and in the worst situation his 'mind goes blank'. (Actually, it doesn't go blank. Quite simply he starts thinking of the audience, not of his speech.)

The remedy for this is: don't panic. Above all, don't look worried. Stay calm as you pick up your thread once more.

Generally, however, silences are golden. The ability to hold a long silence and make it seem natural, is the mark of a gifted speaker, which clearly demonstrates his mastery over the audience.

'He Has A Voice That Makes Him Seem A God'

Your voice should have the capacity to *roll* and *thunder* and *whisper* and *crackle* – all within a few sentences. It should be able to swell and subside, stop short, leap into motion again – with every word clearly enunciated and not a jot of meaning lost.

I am not a purist about voice. Everyone's voice is different, and it would be monstrous to try to force all voices into the same mould. Let there be diversity, colour, interest. But also let everyone's voice be effective. Here are some things that need to be worked on:

Volume. You must have good carrying power to reach the back of a large room. Some speakers are far too quiet, usually because of poor breathing. They breathe too shallowly. Try breathing deeply, ferociously, so that great gusts of air strike your upraised hand. After some practice at this, you can start forming words that will boom out with greatly improved carrying power. And note especially: *the secret of improving voice is to go to the opposite extreme – exaggerate the effect you are trying to achieve. Then, when you stop practising, your voice should settle to a halfway position that is about right.* In this case constantly practise great heaving expulsions of air, then see a gradual improvement in carrying power as your speeches progress. Of course some people are not whisperers but thunderers, and their task is to practise speaking especially quietly to tone down excess of volume. Surging from loud to quiet, in practice, is a good way to reduce your normal speaking volume.

Pace. One of the worst faults is to speak in standard groups of words. You utter eight or ten words; pause; then another eight; pause; then another ten; pause. While pausation is an excellent thing, this is quite the wrong way of doing it and the pauses end up mostly in the wrong places. The fault is bad breathing. Each pause is a quite unconscious halt for breath. Again, the remedy is to practise deep breathing from the belly button until you develop enough breath to carry you through to where the pauses *should* be made.

Another fault of pace is ultra-fast delivery. Often it occurs in people who think especially fast on their feet and who try to make their speech keep up with their thoughts. That's another bad mistake. Slow down. Get the benefits of pausation and also allow your thoughts to slip ahead of your speech, which helps you to shape what is to come. Machine-gun speakers frequently tangle their words, often produce episodic, badly structured speeches, and fail to lodge much of their material with the audience. Remedy: practise speaking very slowly which should reduce your normal rate of delivery. Of course at the other extreme are those who think slowly on their feet, and who punctuate silences with *ums, ers* and *ahs*. This is a very bad habit which results in part from unnecessary anxiety over filling of pauses, and in part from self-consciousness. Forget the fact that you are in front of an audience. Concentrate on the content of your speech, and you will find greater fluency will come naturally.

Pitch. Some speakers deliver in a soporific monotone, a drone that fails to make use of rise and fall in the voice. Others are squeaky or strident or shrill. Still others are rasping, guttural or gravelly. Once again, the remedy is to exaggerate at the opposite extreme – if your voice is high-pitched, practise really low growls. If your voice is too low, practise squeaks. Keep at it and you should find your normal speaking voice will settle somewhere between the extremes. And of course you must vary your delivery to avoid either a high or a low monotone. One failing is to speak from the throat rather than through the teeth. Try to think of it as propelling the words through your teeth rather than sucking them from your throat.

Enunciation. Far too many speakers slur their delivery, run words together, and fail to distinguish word meaning. When enunciated clearly the words *adverse* and *averse* should be clearly distinguishable. So too *allusion* and *illusion*. Don't say *ishee* for *is she,* or *wonday*

81

for *one day* or *gonome* for *gone home*. When words come through un-clearly, the fault is usually bad enunciation. It is caused by poor use of the lips – either the lips are too loose to give control or they are not used enough (ex-President Jimmy Carter must be one of the worst examples of no-lip-movement in the history of language). The remedy is to practise exaggerated lip movements (working the lower jaw vigorously at the same time), with the aim of developing firmness and control. Exaggerate enough and you should settle down to a good in-between level in normal speech. Practise especially the clear sounding of all consonants, particularly the tricky *t's, d's, p's* and *g's*. And practise hitting every syllable clearly on multi-syllable words. Of course, full strong use of lips, lower jaw and teeth will meld in closely with changes of facial expression. Far too many speakers are wooden, unsmiling, even anxious in appearance, and the general immobility of features extends to poor use of lips and lower jaw. Reverse the process: let your face light up. Before the mirror, practise exaggerated expressions and lip move-ments. Develop the feeling of a mobile face.

Aim for the roller-coaster effect. In a speech, words that would be skipped over in conversation are 'dragged out', lengthened, given depth of intonation. The emphasis is not just in volume or stress but in the way all the syllables are deepened, lengthened. 'The *whole* of our *country grieves tonight.*' In conversation this will tend to be a rather flat statement. But in a speech it will take twice as long to say, and there will be a depth of emphasis rolling through the sentence and rounding out the four italicised words.

Most people realise they should stress some words, but go about it the wrong way. They will say the first six words of a sentence in a monotone. Then *wham* the seventh word is stressed. Then *splodge* the next six words are given in a monotone once more. This is a common failing. People emphasise isolated words. Instead, they should speak in groups of words, letting the stresses roll *up* to the key word and *down* again. Think of it as a roller-coaster in which changes in volume are upward and downward sweeps. This is what is known as rise and fall of voice in speech. It can give an almost poetic lilt and cadence to what you are saying. And when combined with good choice of words and correct grammar, it becomes oratorical:

'He is his own worst enemy . . . He carries the mark of doom

. . . He has placed it upon himself . . . And his tragedy is . . . that he is incapable of removing it.' Try these words out loud, in a monotone, stressing an occasional word. Dreadful, isn't it? Now introduce four pauses of different length, the longest of them in the middle of the last sentence. Vary the length of the pauses. Then introduce other tiny pauses, or hesitations, after particular words. Use your lips to form the words roundly and succinctly, use voice volume to give resonance – and marvellous, exquisite pausation to balance the upward and downward sweeps of your roller-coaster delivery.

Pronunciation. This is different from enunciation. You should always try to improve your pronunciation. But I must confess that mild faults do not bother me at all. People from different countries, and from different parts of the same country, pronounce words differently, and this can give spice and interest to their speech (especially when combined with an unusual accent).

It is much more important to develop rhythm and cadence, rise and fall in volume, pausation, and synchronisation of facial expression to words than to produce a perfect Oxford delivery. Remember that a flawless piece of elocution can be the most dreadfully boring speech if it lacks life and colour. But the man with the cracked voice and rough-cut use of words can spin enthralling yarns. So by all means put improved pronunciation on your list of things to work at, but set it low in priority. Other things should come first.

Some Extra Points

About Presentation

Dress. A lot of nonsense is said and written on this subject. Dress neatly and comfortably, and appropriate to the occasion – that's all. It is absurd to insist that a man should always have his jacket done up or that a woman should not wear a slit skirt. It's not what you wear that matters, but how you come across. I once listened to a fabulous speech by an unconventional university student who wore a slouch hat, black singlet, battered trousers and rolled-down gumboots. He held the audience in the palm of his hand from beginning to end.

Practising before a mirror. Never mind that a member of the family

83

may come up behind you and squawk: 'Isn't Polly a pretty boy!' Be relaxed and matter-of-fact about using the mirror to improve your presentation. Don't be surreptitious. Make your own jokes about it. Speaking before a mirror is not an act of vanity: it's part of the patient practice and self-discipline any beginner needs to 'come across well' to an audience. Use the mirror not only to practise gesture but also to practise use of lips and jaw.

Apologising to the audience. Never, never apologise to the audience. If you stumble on a few words, don't say 'I'm sorry' – just put matters right and move on. Apologising damages that air of quiet authority which you as a speaker must try to convey. Also: never thank the audience. It's over to them to thank *you,* by their applause, for giving them your time and effort. Quite the worst way of ending any speech is with the words 'Thank you'. This ruins the final stirring or meaningful words of a carefully constructed dissertation.

When the audience yawns. Yes, some audiences do yawn! But a better indicator that they are bored is that they are not looking at you. If their eyes are cast down, or up to the ceiling or out the window, almost certainly they have drifted off into their own thoughts. This is an extra benefit of eye contact: not only does it establish rapport with the audience, but it tells you, when your eyes are not meeting theirs, that you have lost them. If you have been going a long time, the best thing is to wrap up and come to a quick conclusion. If not, you have to regain your command of the audience. The best way to do this is to change pace. Drop your voice, raise it again. Bring in a dramatic anecdote or a good joke. But *wake them up.* Remember too that if people in the front rows are absorbed while those at the back are looking at the floor, you are just not loud enough to reach the back.

Summary

1. You need to take command, but in the nicest way, so the audience feels secure in your hands.

2. Don't read your speech if it can be avoided; use minimal notes, preferably none at all.

3. Gesture involves the whole of your body, including facial expression.

4. Eye contact is one of the most powerful methods of establishing rapport with your hearers.

5. Pausation is perhaps the single most difficult and rewarding skill of presentation.

6. Your voice must have good volume, pace, pitch and enunciation.

7. Aim for the roller-coaster effect in your voice, raising and lowering volume in broad sweeps.

Part Two

DIFFERENT
SPEAKING
SITUATIONS

Chapter Seven

HOW TO GIVE CONFIDENT
SPEECHES ON SOCIAL OCCASIONS

It really is easy to give a confident, relaxed 'social' speech. First, it is usually short. Second, you always have a receptive audience. And third, there are simple formulae you can learn and adapt to the circumstances.

Yet a surprising number of people agonise over these occasions. They dread 'saying a few words' at a wedding; they take fright at the thought of the speech-making when they retire or change jobs; they invent excuses to avoid proposing a toast; they dodge all manner of duty speeches at clubs and societies they belong to; and they will even ruin their prospects of promotion by ducking invitations by the boss to speak on behalf of the firm.

Let's put a stop to all this right now. Social speeches can be *fun*. All you need is a bit of guidance. In the course of this chapter we will strip the mystery from the subject. We will discuss not only how you can give happy, enjoyable social speeches of your own, but also how you can orchestrate other people's social speeches when you agree (yes, readily agree) to be master of ceremonies at a gathering.

Later we will look at some types of social speech in detail and I will give you formulae to help you with the construction of each type. You will soon see that you need to discover the purpose of your speech, which will probably be to *welcome* someone, *farewell* someone, *congratulate* someone, *thank* someone, *open* some event or make a *presentation*.

But before we discuss specific types of speech, let's consider some of the qualities common to all good social speeches.

The Essentials To Remember
About Social Speeches

First thing to understand is that it is not your show. In most social speeches you will be speaking *on behalf of others*. You will be honouring some person, organisation or event. People commonly fail with social speeches because they forget this point. The occasion belongs to the person they are honouring – to the bride and groom, to the visitor being welcomed, to the employee being farewelled. The speaker must never upstage the main participant. Remember always to be unobtrusive; don't parade your own knowledge; don't steal the guest's thunder; be *sensitive* to the occasion.

The second requirement is warmth and sincerity. Under no circumstances should you say anything that is likely to upset any of your listeners. This is a time for good fellowship, for ignoring defects and smoothing over differences between people. In social speeches you will commonly tell white lies: if the organisers of the event made a hash of things, you will still compliment them on their hard work. If old Jack has become rather irascible as he approached his sixtieth birthday, you will nevertheless dwell on his likable qualities – or invent them if necessary. It is particularly dangerous to sit in judgement ('Jane has shown she can be prickly and some of us have felt the sharp edge of her tongue, but we all recognise her sincerity and devotion to the bowling club . . .'). Attempts to weigh up the good and bad in the person being honoured almost always come unstuck, and cause great embarrassment.

The third thing to remember is the importance of shared experience. This is one of the touchstones of all good public speaking. Remind the audience of past events they have shared with the guest of honour. ('It was Tom who organised that social cricket match at Picton three years ago. And it was Tom who forgot to bring the stumps. And it was Tom who said: "Never mind. We can use apple boxes instead of stumps. Then the batsman can set his beer jug on the box between hits." ') The shared experience can create laughter, or simply a warm feeling of remembrance. Don't ask yourself: 'What shall I say?' Instead, ask yourself: 'What would this audience like to hear?'

When projecting warmth and sincerity, you must put feeling in your voice, maintain eye contact with your listeners, and smile. But more than that, use words of warmth. Beware of cold, aloof expressions. If you say *I must thank,* or *It is my duty to,* or *My task tonight is,* or *I have been given the job of,* you will sound unenthusiastic, even reluctant or antagonistic.

Be sincere and convincing.
- *It is my very great pleasure to propose this toast.*
- *I feel especially honoured to be asked to thank Tom.*
- *I have admired Alice's fine needlework for years so I jumped at this chance to thank her on your behalf for the charity work she has done over the past thirty-five years.*

Avoid clichés: *tower of strength, friend in need, does the work of ten.* The best way to avoid trite statements is to dwell on specifics – recount the achievements or qualities for which the person is being honoured.

It is very bad form to use notes in a social speech. Maybe you can have a slip of paper in your pocket to help you with some complicated details of a person's past history, or the exact words of a citation he once received. This can be drawn out at the appropriate moment, read from, and put away again. But that's all. It is appalling to read a prepared toast or vote of thanks or farewell speech. Though you may well have spent much time working out what you would say, the *appearance* of spontaneity is essential. (Exception: the recipient of a farewell speech, if shy, may have a few notes.)

Humour is desirable, and the audience may expect it, but it is not essential. It should always be warm and light-hearted – *never* cutting, risqué, or crude.

Be brief, and don't get sidetracked. Make just a few points, and make them well. Far too many social speeches lurch about aimlessly as the speaker gropes his or her way through a set of badly prepared ideas.

Don't hurry. Clipped, businesslike or over-earnest delivery is inappropriate to social speeches. Frequent pauses, an air of goodwill, a readiness to respond to interruptions by the audience, and a friendly expression are indispensable.

How to Propose

Toasts

A toast is a statement of good wishes honouring one or more persons, an organisation or an event. It is followed immediately by everyone (except the person being honoured) raising their glass and drinking. Alcohol is usually used for toasting, but it doesn't have to be. Following the toast there is often a reply – but this time no mass imbibing.

Like any other speech, a toast normally has a beginning, a middle and an end. The end is easy. Yet it is often overlooked by speakers who sit down abruptly, leaving it to the master of ceremonies to fill in by asking everyone to rise and drink the toast!

The ending is always much the same:

'Ladies and gentlemen, please ensure your glasses are filled, and drink to the health and happiness of Egbert and Muriel.'

'I ask you to raise your glasses and drink to the success of our campaign.'

'Please stand and toast the good health and many more years of happiness of dear old Dad.'

'I ask you to join with me in this toast to our great friends and rivals of the Kapiti rowing team.'

The shortest toast ever given is five words. It is the loyal toast to Her Majesty Queen Elizabeth II. At functions where this toast is proposed it is always given first. The proposer rises, raises his or her glass, and says, 'Ladies and Gentlemen, The Queen.' Whereupon everyone rises, says 'The Queen', and drinks to her health. There is no reply and by custom the guests do not smoke until after the loyal toast.

Other toasts may be around thirty seconds, but it is more usual for them to be of one to five minutes. Only the most experienced speakers should attempt to propose a toast lasting five to ten minutes – though I have heard one superb wordspinner take twenty enchanting minutes to honour a rival public speaking club.

How long should be the reply to a toast? For the inexperienced, a simple, blushing, 'Thank you very much', is quite acceptable. But usually a reply will be a few sentences, and often two or three minutes. A person replying to a toast of much praise will commonly display, or feign, modesty: 'I couldn't have achieved anything without the loyal support of my committee.' Or, 'This honour should really go to my staff.' Or, 'Your words are very kind, but whatever success I have achieved was only possible through the support and encouragement of my husband.' It is ungracious to reject praise altogether, but it always looks rather nice if you protest that it is over-generous.

Who proposes toasts? Traditionally, men do. Who replies to toasts? Nearly always, men do. I urge you to have none of this. If grandmother wishes to propose the health of the newborn at his christening, she should do so. If the bride wishes to respond to the toast to the bride and groom, she should do so. Similarly, all other traditions are made to be broken. It is usual for an old friend of the family to propose the toast at a silver wedding anniversary. But there's no reason why a relatively new friend shouldn't do so – especially if he is likely to do a better job!

How do you open a toast? There is no limit to the variations:

– *I hope you noticed how quickly I jumped up to propose this toast. That's because I am a pop-up toaster. . . .*
– *I normally hate the idea of proposing a toast. But this is one I am eager to make. For Gretchen is my dearest and lifelong friend. . . .*
– *I am deeply honoured to be asked to propose a toast to our fearless secretary. Of course Jack has been in a lot of hot water lately for his statements in the press, and I know there are* other people *who would dearly love to toast him . . . on the end of a long fork!*
– *In proposing this toast to the bride and groom I am acting under instructions. One set of instructions comes from the groom . . . a quite different set from the bride.*

On formal occasions your first words may be 'Mr Toastmaster [or Madame Toastmistress or Mr Chairman or Madam Chairperson, Mr President, and so on] and ladies and gentlemen'. On less formal occasions you may begin, 'Alastair and Rowena, and dear friends.' But really I prefer to begin without a salutation at all: that's why the preceding openings have none.

Once launched into your toast, stick to a theme, keep to a planned structure without digressing, and lead up to a crisp, confident invitation to everyone to raise their glasses. And make sure you have the name of the person (or persons) you are toasting clearly fixed in your memory!

Your theme may set out the achievements or qualities of the person being toasted, the importance of the occasion, the significance of an event, the pleasures of good fellowship, the value of personal development, or of community work – whatever is appropriate to the occasion.

Don't cram. It is a mistake to try to fit in *everything* that might be said about Jan's career with the firm or about the softball team's unbeaten record for the season. Pick a few highlights, an interesting or amusing anecdote, and string them together in a concise, orderly manner. If you find at the end, after everyone has raised their glasses, that you've forgotten something vital, don't add a post-script ('Oh by the way, I forgot to say . . .'). That's disastrous. Instead, write down the stray piece of information and give it to the Master of Ceremonies or chairman to announce. Failing that, wait a while, rise again and make the extra announcement yourself.

A Silver (Or Golden) Wedding Anniversary. This is a time for looking back on long years of happy marriage, of friendships, of family ties, of achievements, and of a full and rewarding life. The toast, usually but not necessarily given by an old family friend, might go like this:

How often have we heard it said: 'If I could have my life over, I would do things differently.' Tonight we honour two dear friends, Alick and Joanne, whose thoughts we can easily read. We know that if they were to start life again they would want to spend it in each other's company. The only change they would make would be to marry earlier. Tonight they celebrate their silver wedding anniversary. But the evening is not theirs alone. It belongs also to three lovely children, Aidan and Bettina and Pearl. Plus two exquisite grandchildren, Cherie and Louisa. The list does not stop there. For this evening belongs also in some degree to the rest of us, friends through long years of Alick and Joanne. We have participated in their marriage, and we have been enriched by their friendship, wisdom, good humour and affection. Tonight we bring our warm good wishes to you, our dear friends, and wish you many long years of health and happiness . . . Would everyone now please raise their glasses and drink with me a toast to the happy couple.

Remember that sincerity and warmth are essential. Since you are very likely an old friend of the family, trade on your knowledge:

I have been lucky enough to have known Pop and Annabel all of their married lives. It amazes me to think how they have changed in those twenty-five years. I have watched them grow in wisdom and insight, each enlarging the understanding of the other. What I have learned from them is tolerance, consideration, respect, goodwill and kindness. Indeed, I have never known Annabel say an unkind word about anyone. I have also never known Pop say an unkind word about anyone . . . except the Prime Minister, the tax-man, football referees, and the next-door neighbour's dog!

Then make reference to specific events in their lives, perhaps to ways they have helped their friends and have partaken in the affairs of the community. Finally:

We congratulate Pop and Annabel on reaching their twenty-fifth anniversary and look forward to sharing their fiftieth with them. But when I consider how many friends they have gathered over these twenty-five years I can't imagine how the friends of fifty years will be accommodated in anything smaller than the town hall . . . . I ask you now to rise and drink to the continuing good health and great happiness of Pop and Annabel.

Where the couple is elderly, perhaps celebrating their golden wedding, it is especially appropriate to initiate a mass display of affection. You can begin your toast:

Hands up all the men in the audience who are secretly in love with Alice.

A forest of hands will rise.

And hands up all the women in the audience who are secretly in love with Carl.

Another forest of hands will shoot up.

Then you can begin talking about the extended family of relatives and friends who surround the couple with warmth and affection. You can quote the loving comments a grandchild made about Grandma and Granddad. You can recount humorous anecdotes from the past, and episodes of which the couple are especially proud. Above all, give specific examples that are familiar to all or most of the audience so that a feeling of sharing is built up.

The reply? Traditionally it is given by the husband, but it can be given by husband or wife or both. A brief statement is perfectly appropriate:

Dear friends, we are overwhelmed. We cannot express how much you have all contributed to our happiness over the years. Thank you so much for your kind wishes, your lovely gifts, and above all for being with us on this special day.

If you wish to say more, it is a good practice to pick out some of the points made in the toast and respond to them, or counterpoint them with stories of your own. If there was humour in the toast that went over well, be sure to repeat it (and enlarge it if possible).

To The Bride And Groom. This toast expresses the pleasure of the assembled guests at the marriage of a relative or friend, and their good wishes for the future health and happiness of the newly-weds. It is commonly proposed by an old friend of one of the families.

The toast is usually livened by humour, but this is not essential. It might go like this:

A few weeks ago I received an unusual envelope in my mail. It smelt faintly of roses. With trembling hands I opened it. Could scented paper be the latest trick of the bill collector . . .? Instead, I found an invitation – to attend Nicola's wedding. My first reaction was the somewhat indignant thought that no man could be good enough to marry my favourite niece. Then I was informed that Bob has just joined the Cheltenham basketball team, which is absolutely my favourite team . . . and I began to wonder whether Nicola could be good enough for him . . . I suppose you all got the same invitation to this wedding. Did you notice the strange code letters at the bottom? RSVP. Now I am not very knowledgeable about weddings and things, and that peculiar inscription threw me into a bit of a panic. What could it mean? I decided to ask Aunt Ada. She looked at me as if I was silly and said: 'RSVP? It means Reply Soon Vith Present.' . . . So I replied soon vith present and for my pains I was invited to propose this toast. To do so is, I assure you, one of the greatest pleasures of my life. I have known Nicola since she was a baby. I have watched her grow, not just physically, but in character, in personality, in intelligence, wit and charm. She is truly my favourite person! About Bob I know very little, except that since Nicola chose him he must be a man of remarkable qualities. It will be my pleasure, and the pleasure of all those on Nicola's side of the family, to get to know Bob much better in the years to come. Equally, it will be the pleasure of all those on Bob's side of the family, to learn more about Nicola. And of course many of you here today are already lucky enough to be friends of them both.

Having got this far, you may wish to say something about marriage. As an institution marriage seems under threat, yet it will always endure; marriage is said to be a lottery, yet few people buy their tickets blindly trusting to luck; marriage is a contract in which you should expect no refunds and no trading in on a new model.

Anecdotes can be helpful, but keep them within the bounds of good taste. This is an important day for the bride and groom, and they won't thank you for trivialising it.

The reply is usually given by the bridegroom, who will thank the proposer of the toast for his kind comments; thank everyone for coming and for their gifts; say how lucky he is; thank his parents for their love and help and the example they have provided; say something nice about the bride's parents; make a couple of fond remarks about the bride herself; and comment that, whatever lies in store for them, he and his wife will be able to face any difficulty strengthened by the support of their friends. Often the bridegroom will end his reply by proposing a brief further toast to the bridesmaids. He will comment on how lovely they look, thank them for assisting his wife, and for their friendship to her. He will end by asking the assembly to drink to their health.

Christening. 'We are all witness to new beginning. This wee mite is a bundle of promise. The opportunities for her are limitless. But whatever she achieves in life we hope, and we know, she will be like her parents, in personal qualities and in attitudes. Her upbringing is in good hands. I invite you all to drink to the health, happiness and bright future of baby Gweneth.' A response is not essential but a parent may wish to reply on behalf of the baby.

Twenty-first Birthday. 'Today is the day, in theory at least, when Robert receives the key of the door. I mentioned that to his father and he said, "Humpf. Robert's had the key of the door since he was sixteen – and the key of the car for just as long." ' Refer to his fine family, happy personality, sporting and scholastic achievements, career plans, his interests. The future of the world lies with young people like him – and clearly that future is in good hands. Drink to his health and his future. Robert's reply will normally be one of thanks – to everyone for coming to the party, parents for all they have done. Plus special thanks to his friends and how much he will appreciate their continuing friendship in the years to come.

Absent Friends. This makes brief reference to friends and associates scattered across the world who cannot be present for the occasion. It is appropriate to mention one or two notable absentees by name. 'We are grateful that the ideals and traditions of our club have been spread afar by our friends, but we are sorry they cannot be with us on this happy occasion. Ladies and gentlemen, I give you a toast to our absent friends.'

The Club or the School. Make reference to its traditions, how it 'brought all of us together', forged lasting bonds, loyalty to common ideals, sporting and intellectual challenges, good fellowship, stimulated a spirit of give and take. Anecdotes are especially welcome in such a toast, the more notorious the better. Any well-known episode, however often it has been recounted, will produce a better response than an episode known only to you.

Farewelling An Employee

The speech of farewell may be given by the managing director, a middle-level executive, a foreman or forewoman or a section head. It is usual to say when the employee joined the firm, what positions he or she has held, how highly his or her work has been valued, how his or her colleagues have liked him, how much he or she will be missed, and how great are everyone's good wishes for his or her future.

As in all social speeches the first rule is: you must not embarrass anyone, especially the person being farewelled. There must be no reference whatever to faults or failings. Resist any attempt to weigh up the departing employee's good and bad features ('Jane and I didn't always see eye to eye . . .'). I have heard some quite wretched attempts to do this and without exception they fail.

Even the mildest suggestion of criticism is forbidden. First, as a matter of simple courtesy. Second, because the departing employee is likely to be very nervous. Third, because he or she may well have staunch friends on the staff. Fourth, because the staff should work always in the comfortable certainty that employees are treated at all times with courtesy, consideration and respect.

Your job then is to dwell on good points, ignoring the bad.Here then, is what you might say:

Today is a sad day for us all. We lose a friend and one of the best foremen we have ever had. I am sure that in future we will pause from time to time when wrestling with a problem and will ask: 'What would Antoine have done?' Or, 'What advice would he have given us if he were still here?' Antoine has been with us twelve years. He started as a bench hand, and pro- gressed to foreman in remarkably short time. He has built up a first class crew of people who all respect him for his fairness, his willingness to listen, his hard work, his good humour, his helpfulness, and his thorough under- standing of the job. Now the time has come for him to move on to new chal- lenges. We have mixed feelings. For the one part we are very sorry to see him leave, but for the other we are conscious of the great opportunity he will have in his demanding new position, and we are confident he will excel in it.

Where the departing employee is retiring, your farewell speech will wish him or her well in his leisure years. If his or her retirement plans are known, you may make reference to them. You will also couple the wife or husband in your best wishes for their joint retirement.

Whether the employee is leaving to retire or to go to a new job, the farewell speech will commonly run over some highlights of his time with the firm ('Bob will always remember the trauma of the big shift to these premises when all his stock-records went missing for three weeks') and recall one or two humorous episodes ('I still recall the day we replaced the tea-lady with a machine, and Bob dressed the machine in a skirt and blouse'). These need not have involved the departing employee. Remember to be unhurried, warm, smiling and sincere. Be specific where you can – mention ideas and methods of the departing employee that will continue to benefit the firm in the future.

You will end by producing the farewell card and the gift. If well chosen, the farewell card will contain a message worth reading out. Better still, if the card has been made by the staff, there will be several parts you can read out.

Finally comes the handshake and the passing over of the gift: 'Sally, on behalf of all the staff I ask you to accept this farewell gift with our thanks and our warmest best wishes for the future.'

In replying, a shy person may wish to be very brief. 'I am deeply touched. The only thing I can say is: thank you all and I shall miss you very much.' But it is not difficult to do a little more. Start with remarks about the farewell card, then turn to the gift. 'Let's begin by opening this magnificent package.' Take your time. If the opening is difficult, someone will help you. When the present is revealed, say how much you like it and how you will treasure it and how it will remind you of them all. Then pause, look around the faces of your assembled colleagues, and thank them sincerely. 'Someone has put a lot of thought into choosing this gift and a lot of people have gone to much trouble in making up this farewell card. I'm going to miss you all. I shall also miss the friendship, fun and happy atmosphere.' Thank the organisation for contributing to your training and personal development. Make special thanks where appropriate: 'I would never have got into computer programming if it hadn't been for the help and encouragement of Bill Tickers.' Thank your colleagues generally for their helpfulness and friendship. Refer to one or two interesting and humorous episodes from your time with the firm – but keep them concise and don't allow yourself to stray from the main theme of your speech. You can end by saying you will continue to take an interest in the progress of the firm and will drop in from time to time for a cup of coffee. 'Once again, thank you all and bless you.'

How To Introduce
A Speaker

Speeches of introduction are probably more often botched than any other kind. The worst crime is to make pronouncements of your own about the speaker's subject. Carry *that* too far and you run the risk that he will rise, stonily inform the audience 'There is nothing I can usefully add to what has already been said,' and sit down again!

When introducing a speaker, you must get his name right, including the precise pronunciation. (And don't forget to *use* his name at the end of your introduction!) You must also know his qualifications and experience, the position he holds and the exact title of his address. Try *not* to run through a dry catalogue of dates: when he was born, where he went to school, the positions he has held. Instead, make his background come alive:

Mr Chairman, ladies and gentlemen. Inflation accounting is one of the most controversial issues in management today. And our guest speaker, Professor Walker Higginbotham, is one of those who have made it so. I doubt he could ever have thought, back in the 1930s when he was a student at Oxford, that our economy would see the raging hyper-inflation that bedevils it today. Professor Higginbotham developed his economic theories lecturing in Montreal and in Sydney, during a stint with the World Bank, and while working with a multi-national company. Now as Professor of Economics at the University of the South Pacific he is one of the world's foremost enthusiasts for inflation accounting. In his address today, Professor Higginbotham will tell you why he believes inflation accounting, also known as current cost accounting, is essential to give a true picture of the finances of any business. He will argue that many businesses which profess to be making satisfactory profits are in fact running at a loss because they are not making adequate provision for replacement of equipment at tomorrow's inflated prices. Ladies and gentlemen, Professor Walker Higginbotham.

Don't overpraise the speaker (that may panic him!). Generalisations, such as 'brilliant', 'hilariously funny', 'one of the greatest botanists in the world' tend to sound insincere, and to be unsettling to the speaker. It is far better to be specific about his position, his achievements and his major views and theories. Remember, it's partly your job to 'soften up' the audience, to prepare the way for the guest speaker and help get the audience in a receptive mood. A rambling, uncoordinated introduction will be a handicap, not a help, to the guest speaker.

So be crisp, and whet the audience's appetite for what is to come. Speak to the assembly, *not* to the guest speaker. The only time you turn to look at him is at the end – 'Ladies and gentlemen, Professor Walker Higginbotham.'

The Vote Of Thanks
To A Speaker

Again, this is often done abysmally. Your job is not only to thank the speaker on behalf of the audience, but also to crystallise her message. You must convey warmth, and thank her sincerely. The speaker has given her time and effort, and courtesy demands that she be thanked properly.

A good vote of thanks can win over the audience in a way the speaker herself may have been unable to do. The warmth of your thanks, and the reasoning you use, may convert a dissatisfied audience into a grudgingly grateful one.

You may show that the speaker's views, however unpalatable to her listeners, do have merit, are sincerely held, and enlarge everyone's understanding of the subject by presenting an opposing point of view.

Or you may have picked out the speaker's message more clearly than the audience, simply because you concentrated on it. If you can summarise the speaker's message more clearly than she expressed it (she may be inexperienced), you can change the audience's attitude to the speaker and to the speech they have just heard.

Above all, you must look for the major threads in the speech you are listening to. Those are the points you will pick out in your vote of thanks before asking the audience to show their appreciation by applauding.

There is *no* reply to a vote of thanks. The speaker should smile modestly and stare into her lap!

How To Be A Good
Master Of Ceremonies

The job of Master of Ceremonies (or toastmaster) is a jazzed-up version of that of chairman. The M.C. introduces a series of speakers throughout a programme, saying a few words about each, and generally keeping the proceedings moving with a light touch and crisp, good-humoured control.

As soon as you agree to be an M.C., you must sit down with the organisers (the parents of the bride for a wedding, the chairman of the organising committee for a banquet) and find out what they want. If they are in doubt, be prepared to advise them. You will need to know the toast list and discover the competence or otherwise of the speakers. Speaking times will need to be worked out for each person. Ideally, you should chat in advance with each speaker to discover roughly what he intends saying – to avoid duplication of material, and to veto unacceptable jokes. You will also need to know the composition of the audience.

On the night itself you will be thoroughly prepared, with the order and timing of speakers written down (this may also be given on the printed programme). You will also have your own notes on each speaker and the punchlines of the various jokes you propose using.

Delegate heavily. Give reliable people the task of looking after the seating arrangements, checking microphones, meeting the important guests and the speakers, and so on. If you think that one of your speakers may drink too much before he speaks, delegate someone to keep an eye on him.

At the outset you will chat briefly with each of the speakers. If they are not at the top table, make sure you know where they are seated.

Open the proceedings on time. Normally the M.C. himself makes the speech of welcome. Since you will be trying to establish a feeling of shared experience, you may decide to make special mention of some of the participants. 'Hands up all those from the Alpha Club [or from Jamestown, or from the Prentice family]. Let's all give a big hand to the people from Alpha.'

It is not essential to be humorous, but you should try to have a few good one-liners. And be prepared to pick up comments from the audience and from the speakers themselves. Be crisp, confident and brief when introducing each speaker. Remember: their speeches are the main events. Your job is to be the smooth link-person who holds everything together.

Don't hesitate to stimulate the audience: 'Are you all having a good time?'

'Yes,' they will respond.

'Louder,' you insist.

'Yes,' they shout.

'It must be the booze,' you say, rolling your eyes to the ceiling.

Don't rush. It is especially important to be relaxed. Keep your movements slow, smile, cast your gaze around the audience. Don't worry about little gaps in the proceedings – people will fill them in naturally with conversation. During these gaps you can stroll into the audience and chat to your next speaker, letting him know he will be on in, say, five minutes.

On some occasions the M.C. will need to perform extra duties – like leading everyone into 'Happy Birthday' or 'For She's A Jolly Good Fellow' after the guest of honour has responded to the main toast. This little piece of off-key minstrelsy nicely covers up what can be an awkward moment when a nervous guest of honour stumbles to the end of her reply.

Summary

1. Be graceful and genial. Smile. Be relaxed and unhurried.

2. Convey warmth and sincerity. Never embarrass anyone.

3. Remember it is not your show. Make the guest of honour the centre of attention.

4. Be brief. Tie your comments into a theme.

5. Humour is desirable, but not essential.

6. In replying to a toast or vote of thanks, try to pick up some of the points already made. Add an anecdote or a dash of humour.

7. Involve the audience whenever possible.

Chapter Eight

HOW SPEAKING SKILLS CAN
BOOST YOUR CAREER

At one time in your life above all others you need to communicate well: when being interviewed for the job you really want. When you walk into that unfamiliar office, shake hands with one or more strangers, and lower yourself into that strategically placed chair, you will need special speaking skills to do well.

It's called a job interview, but when properly done it's much more than that. For you, it is an exercise in shrewd salesmanship; for the interviewer, it is a sceptical, probing analysis. To neither of you do the skills come naturally. It takes experience, practice and training.

In this chapter we will discuss interview techniques: how to present yourself well, the preparation you must do, how to deal with trap questions, the things you are likely to be asked, how to read the progress of the interview, what you should ask, and whether to accept the job when it is offered. We will discuss also the ways in which speaking skills can help you when you are in your job.

The advice given here will be most useful to men and women in middle to senior management positions. Although school-leavers and more junior staff may find some of it valuable, their requirements cover a different range of skills. A separate book would be necessary to deal with their situation adequately.

Let Years Of Preparation
Strengthen Your Quest

If you are serious about your career, you should study interview techniques as thoroughly as you would study any academic subject or new skill. It is futile to wait years for the chance to apply for your dream job – and then hope to beat off all other applicants with inspiration and good intentions alone. Some of your rivals will be tough, battle-hardened veterans. They will know how to recognise a structured interview; an unstructured interview; a stress interview. They will know how to respond to closed questions and open questions; how to deal with silence when it is used as a tactic; how to avoid being drawn into damaging admissions; how to assist an inexperienced interviewer.

So, how should you train yourself to be good at interviews? First, by reading widely: not only books written to assist the applicant, but also those written to help the interviewer. Two good books are *Getting a New Job* (Consumers' Association, London); and *Getting the Job You Want* by Howard Dowding and Sheila Boyce (Ward Lock, London). But don't just go on a reading binge. As the years pass, read steadily and widely, and your understanding will deepen: your understanding of how to write a letter of application; how to handle the interview; when to accept and when to reject a job offer.

Second, practice. Apply for jobs. Even when you are doubtful that you are interested in the particular vacancy. A young person who is raw and untutored should try to obtain three or four interviews a year, simply to improve his interview technique. Older people who have not been interviewed for years, but want a change of job, should start firing off applications just to brush up on their interview skills. Don't be alarmed that you may be offered a job you don't want. It builds your self-confidence to turn down job offers that do not meet your needs.

How To Prepare
For An Interview

This long-term training in interview skills is part of your self-development. When you are called for the interview that really matters, you will be able to prepare for it calmly, bolstered by experience, knowledge and skill.

First, if a full job description is not offered, you will ask for one. Then you will want to find out as much as possible about the company or organisation. You will get its annual reports for the past several years, plus any brochures or other publications it puts out. Not only will these documents tell you what the company does, but also whether it is financially sound, and if so whether it is expanding or stagnant.

During the interview, you will want to probe these points

further, and especially to ask about the department, section or division you would join: is it developing or contracting; is its budget rising; when was it last reorganised; is it meeting its objectives; what problems does it face; what is the level of staff turnover; for how long was your predecessor in the job; what staff training is given; what methods of staff appraisal are used; what is the promotion system? You may find answers to some of these questions before the interview; the others will have to wait.

The rest of your preparation will be of two kinds: (a) studying and memorising the requirements of the position; (b) identifying and memorising your skills and strengths, along with frank but *positively worded* answers about your weaknesses and about blots on your record.

Go over your notes repeatedly in the days before the interview. In this way you should be prepared for maybe two-thirds or more of the questions you will be asked.

Don't expect to ad-lib. Put yourself in the interviewer's place. Think his thoughts, adopt his attitude. What will he want to know? How will he disguise his intentions? What should you seek to communicate even if not asked? This technique of thinking the other fellow's thoughts will be developed in Chapters 10, 11 and 12. Become good at it.

Be positive. Put down your qualifications on paper. Head it: *Why I Am The Right Person For This Job*. Start with the requirements as given in the advertisement and job description. Alongside each, set out the ways in which you meet the requirement, with examples. Work out your most important and most relevant skills, qualifications and experience. How do they fit you for this job? If you are asked what you like least about your present job, how will you answer – for maybe the things you dislike are a necessary part of the new job? How should you respond when asked what your weaknesses are? How can you present them positively? Likewise, can you turn defects in your past record into pluses? Be ready to say why you left each of your previous jobs – and make the reason positive, not negative.

Be candid with yourself about your personal qualities. Do you display initiative; come up with practical, well-thought-out ideas; react calmly in a crisis; meet deadlines without reminders; analyse problems to decide what solutions are possible and the advantages and disadvantages of each; use your time well; pay rigorous attention to accuracy and detail; finish every job; cope well with several tasks at once?

It's no use simply answering *Yes* to each of these questions. In any event, a good interviewer will not ask the questions directly, but will extract the truth from you in a roundabout way. Your task is to find *examples* from your past history that demonstrate your good qualities. It is not enough to assert that you have them: you must provide evidence. Instead of 'Yes, I can handle myself well in a crisis', give an example. 'Last year a consumer organisation tested our electric toaster and pronounced it highly dangerous. It was my job to decide if this finding was true, and advise the company what to do. Can I tell you how I went about it?'

Make no mistake: half the secret in interviewing well lies in the preparation. Broadly, the interviewer wants to discover two things: (a) what qualities you possess that may fit you for this position; and (b) how you handle yourself when giving that information.

On The Day Itself

Get plenty of sleep the night before. On the big day ensure you arrive in abundant time. Take no risk that you may arrive late, *or* breathless and flustered. Have with you your list of the job's requirements and your qualifications. While waiting to be called, take out that list and run over the main points again. By the time you enter the interview room, those items will be fresh in your mind.

Inside the room, beware. Regrettably, many interviewers reject applicants on first impressions. If a person is nervous, flustered, looks at the floor, has a weak or sweaty handshake, wears cowboy boots or heavy makeup, sits before being invited to, enters carrying a knapsack, or commits any of a hundred minor sins – the interviewer may switch off immediately.

Be sure you are dressed neatly, comfortably and conservatively. Keep your movements slow and deliberate. Shake hands firmly. Look the interviewer in the eye; if there is a panel, let your gaze rove calmly over them. Sit when asked to, or when everyone else has done so. Don't be the first to speak. Pause before answering. Use the interviewer's name – but not first name. Don't slouch. Jerky movements or over-eagerness betray nervousness, and while that does not rule you out for some jobs, inevitably it mars the impression you give. Be alert and attentive. Smile. Try to look relaxed and confident. When challenged, stick to your views in a friendly way. Don't swear or use colloquialisms. Never lie – but don't volunteer information that may be damaging to you.

The Three Types
Of Interview

Interviews may be (a) structured, (b) unstructured, (c) pressure.

A structured (or planned) interview proceeds according to a set pattern. Often it is in three parts: you are told something about the job; you are asked a series of interlocking questions; then you are invited to ask your own questions.

An unstructured (or rambling) interview tends to be rather off-the-cuff. This happens often when there is a panel of interviewers – unless they decide beforehand what matters they want to cover and divide up the questions. Because there is no plan, the interviewer, or panel, often ends up with an incomplete picture of some or all of the applicants.

A pressure (or stress) interview seeks to put you under threat, even to insult you, with the idea of finding out how you perform under fire. The interviewer will disagree with you, seek to unsettle you, to see whether you stick calmly to your opinions, or back down in consternation.

Let's look more closely at each type of interview:

1. In a structured interview, the questions will often be grouped under six or seven headings: your education and family background; your experience and skills; your motivation and ambitions; your achievements; your intelligence and personal qualities as shown at the interview; your leisure interests and community involvement; your health and physical strength.

For some jobs one class of questions will be more important than any other – say, health, physical strength and manual dexterity. For other jobs the interviewer will concentrate on a different class of questions – say, personal qualities such as tact, patience, judgement and ability to placate warring unions. When preparing for your interview, try to work out which set of questions is likely to be most important.

2. In an unstructured interview, you may have to be persistent to

insert information about yourself into the flow of unrelated or ir-relevant questions. When you can see the interviewer is grass-hoppering, try to group your answers so that they build a picture of your good qualities. After answering one question, ask the inter-viewer: 'Would you like to hear about the way I reorganised my firm's record-keeping system?' Or: 'May I tell you about the course in statistical method I took last year?' Keep pushing out information about your qualifications, skills, achievements, ambitions.

3. The pressure interview disconcerts many applicants, as it is in-tended to. The interviewer asks you a question and as soon as you have answered, he says tersely: 'I think you are wrong.' Then he waits to see if you will withdraw your statement in confusion. If you ask him why he thinks you are wrong, he will deliver a blunt and uncomplimentary rejection of your evidence or argument, or both. Again he will wait for your response. Don't be dismayed. In asking these unfriendly questions, the interviewer is not upset with you. He is detached and unemotional. He knows what stresses the job will place on you if you are appointed, and he wants to know how you will perform under pressure. So stay calm, and stick to your views, restating them firmly and rationally.

Often an interview will proceed along structured lines until the three-quarter mark – then *wham,* it becomes a stress interview. This can be highly unsettling if you have thought you were doing well, and then suddenly are told: 'That's crazy. If you acted that way our clients would resign in droves.' Be prepared at all stages of the inter-view for a sudden chill to descend. This can happen in the friendliest atmosphere. Don't panic. The interviewer has no reason to quarrel with you. His sudden unfriendliness is a tactic. Stay calm, pause, and think your way through his frosty question.

What do interviewers hope to find in you? It depends on the type of job – but for nearly all jobs, they are looking for someone who is friendly, cheerful, relaxed, positive, sincere, frank, thoughtful, alert. They look for enthusiasm, determination to succeed, an interest in the requirements of the job, good manners, and thorough preparation.

What interviewers do not like in an applicant is indifference, negative attitudes, shyness, nervousness, lack of confidence, a complaining attitude, low ambition, poor initiative, a chip on the shoulder, bad manners, excessive interest in money or status.

How Much Do You Say?

If you say too little, the interviewer will never know enough about you to appoint you.

If you say too much, you risk telling him something that will cause him to reject you.

The skill is to pitch yourself between the extremes: to give measured, balanced replies – preferably using words you have rehearsed. Above all, know when to stop. Even people who are normally somewhat reserved can babble from a combination of tension and eagerness to get the job.

Much depends on the way the interviewer frames his questions. As far as possible interviewers should use open questions that encourage the applicant to give expansive replies. They should avoid closed questions that push the applicant towards brief (especially *Yes* or *No*) answers.

Closed questions often begin with such words as: *can you, did you, do you, are you, which, when, who.*

Open questions often begin with such words as: *why, tell me about, what, how, give me examples, explain to me.*

In the following pairs, (a) is closed and (b) is open:

(a) *Did you enjoy university?*
(b) *What did you like most about university and why?*

(a) *Can you use a personal computer?*
(b) *How much do you know about computers?*

(a) *Do you keep your cool in a crisis?*
(b) *Tell me about the worst problem you have faced in the last year and how you handled it.*

When faced with a closed question, try to avoid a short response. Expand your answer by giving examples (not general statements). If asked, 'Can you use a personal computer', you might reply: 'Yes. In fact I own one. I use it for my own financial records. I also use it to help my wife, who sells bamboo curtains, to do cost estimates for customers. Last year I took a course in computer programming at night school. Would you like to hear more about that course?'

Open questions need more care. First, they can easily be turned into closed questions. If asked 'What are your ambitions?' You might reply: 'Well, I don't suppose I have any.' That answer would be disastrous. But equally, don't go too far in the opposite direction by fixing the interviewer with a steely eye and declaring: 'In five years I would expect to be in your job – having helped you to rise higher still.' That's an unwise answer because it assumes the interviewer's ambitions are as strong as yours! A good, balanced reply would be: 'I'm keen to develop my skills and I think two or three years in this job would fit me for more responsibility, hopefully with this firm. In due course, I would like to be sales manager of a medium to large company.' Nice, safe stuff that displays evidence of ambition without threatening the interviewer.

Another type of question can be very tricky: the hypothetical question. 'If you got this job and the printer's staff went on strike three days before your new sales brochure was due to be launched, what would you do?'

The interviewer of course knows this problem well, and has his own pet answer. As an outsider, you cannot be expected to provide a solution as well as you would do after some experience in the job. Yet the interviewer unreasonably expects you to give the 'right' answer at a moment's notice. A better question would have been: 'Tell me of a crisis you faced in your present job and how you overcame it.' Then you would be answering from experience, and the interviewer could judge your *general* ability to solve problems.

So when faced with a hypothetical question ('What would you do if . . .'), you would do well to reply: 'I would want to know all the facts of the situation before I could give an answer. Instead, I wonder if I could tell you of the kind of problem I am used to solving and how I go about it? That would tell you something about my skills in problem-solving.' In this way, you keep to familiar ground, and to material you have rehearsed during your preparation for the interview.

Leading questions are a lucky gift. A poor interviewer will ask: 'What do you feel about working over-time?' The applicant, having been shown what the interviewer wants to hear, immediately responds: 'Don't mind it at all.' Or the interviewer may ask: 'From time to time a customer may come in very irate and tear strips off you because some little thing has gone wrong with his order. How do you think you would react in that situation?' Obvious answer: 'I am used to such upsets. I would listen calmly and then sort out what to do to fix his problem and use some sweet talk to get him back on our side.'

111

Silence As A Tactic

To the inexperienced interviewer or applicant silence is uncomfortable. Each rushes to fill it. A raw interviewer will talk long-windedly about the requirements of the job, ignoring the fact that he should be finding out about the applicant. While normally the applicant would not interrupt, you may have to in order to sell yourself.

Experienced interviewers go to the opposite extreme. They use silence to draw from the applicant information she has schooled herself not to give. Often a lengthening silence will bring tumbling forth damaging admissions which no applicant need volunteer.

Interviewer: 'Why did you leave Tar and Feathers Ltd?'
Applicant: 'I wanted to broaden my skills – felt I was in a dead end.'
Interviewer: 'Nothing else?' *Long pause.*
Applicant: 'Not really.' *Further long pause.*
Applicant: 'Well actually, I didn't much like the boss either.'
Further long pause. The interviewer looks friendly enough, but simply says nothing. The applicant feels the pressure mounting. Suddenly she blurts out all she shouldn't.
Applicant: 'The boss never cared about the staff. He was always pulling me up over little things. Sometimes if I was a bit late for work he was very niggly. Then he didn't give me a promotion, but others got it. It was very unfair. I used to take work home. I couldn't help it if I was overloaded all the time. I should have been given more assistance.'

Whether Tar and Feathers were fair or unfair employers is beside the point: this company is unlikely to risk hiring someone who clearly was found unsatisfactory in a previous job. Using silence, the interviewer has deftly extracted that information.

Be strong. When silences lengthen, let them lengthen. Remain calm, and do not be drawn into quick ill-considered statements. You will find after a while the interviewer will realise there is no point trying to weaken your self-control: very probably, he will admire it.

How To Answer Those
Often-Asked Questions

Expect to be asked these questions, and have your answer ready:

1. 'Why do you want to leave your present job?'

Unwise answers: *I want more money; I am fed up with the way they treat their staff; they don't appreciate me; it is a dead-end job; I don't like working overtime.*

A good answer: *I don't want to leave my job. I'm happy in it and doing well. But I realise I need new challenges and further opportunity for development. The job you have advertised would be an important new step in my career.*

2. 'Why do you want this job?'

Unwise answers: *I'm not certain yet that I want it; my girlfriend works here; the pay looks good; it's near my home; I think I need a change.*

A good answer: *I've always admired this company. I like its record of success and the brilliant way it launched its new Blue Vegetables line. I feel this company can give me experience and skills I would be unlikely to get elsewhere. I like the way the company encourages initiative and bestows more responsibility - that's what I want.*

3. 'What makes you think you would fit into this position?'

Unwise answers: *Because it is just like the one I am in now; I get on well with people and can fit in anywhere; frankly I can do this job on my ear; I've never had any difficulty in any of my jobs so far.*

A good answer: *From the advertisement and job description I believe there are six main requirements of the position. They are: intelligence, initiative, problem-solving skills, steadiness under pressure, ability to meet deadlines and a thorough knowledge of screenprinting techniques. I believe I fill each of these requirements for the following reasons . . .*

4. 'What are your strong points?'

Unwise answers: *I think I'm a good all-rounder; I've never had a day sick in my life; I know how to follow orders; I never accept that I'm beaten.*

A good answer: *I like people and get on well with them. I'm a team person and I don't try to hog all the credit. I can set priorities, work to objectives, and meet deadlines. I am thorough, painstaking and fanatical in the pursuit of highest quality. I guess you could say I'm a perfectionist. I really do get satisfaction from doing a job well.*

5. 'What are your weak points?'

Unwise answers: *To be perfectly frank, I don't really think I have any; I suppose I don't suffer fools gladly; I can't stand my boss breathing down my neck; on rare occasions I lose my cool.*

A good answer: *I'm always cautioning myself not to be too impatient, and to realise not everyone can work at my pace. I guess impatience to get things done is one of my worst faults. I also find myself tempted to criticise* poor work, and again I have to warn myself to be tactful.

6. 'How do you react when you think your boss is wrong?'

Unwise answer: *He's the boss, so if he's listened to me and doesn't agree, I'll accept that.*

A good answer: *No two people agree with each other more than 70 per cent of the time. So it's natural if my boss and I disagree on 30 per cent of occasions, and it's nothing to get excited about. However, if I can't convince my boss on an important matter, and still feel I'm correct, I reserve the right to come back later with a better argument.*

Other good statements:

– *I want to learn and develop new skills.*

– *I want people to tell me if I make mistakes and help me to improve.*

– *I don't believe in being a lone wolf.*

– *I don't bring problems to my boss – I bring him alternative solutions with the arguments for and against each alternative, plus my recommendation.*

– *I want the chance to be creative; to do a job that gives me stimulation and satisfaction.*

– *I want responsibility and recognition for my achievements.*

– *Salary doesn't worry me. I know my abilities and I am confident my boss will reward those abilities fairly.*

– *I dislike excessive supervision, boredom, sloppy work, negative thinking.*

How To Handle Those
Blots On Your Record

Always make a positive answer when asked about defects in your work record or background. Here are some of the tricky questions you may be asked, and examples of how to turn your answer into a positive statement.

1. 'Were you ever fired?'

Yes. It was quite some time ago, when I was in the wrong job and didn't know where I was going. It did me a lot of good and I have been on a good career track ever since.

2. 'Why were you a filing clerk so long?'

That was a real learning period. Not only did I get good at my job, but I found out how an organisation really works. I didn't mark time – it was a period of valuable development.

3. 'Why have you changed jobs so often?'

I've seen other people get into the wrong groove and stick there too long, ruining their careers. So I wanted to try a lot of things to understand better what opportunities are available. Now I have decided firmly on salesmanship – and the variety of jobs I have held gave me width of experience to complement the depth of experience I now hope to gain in the selling side of things.'

4. 'What about this gap in your career?'

Quite simply, I made a stupid mistake. I ended up in prison. That taught me a lesson I will never forget. I think I am a better person now that I have been through that traumatic experience.

When preparing for the interview, spend half your time clarifying your strengths and how to emphasise them – and the other half time identifying your weaknesses, and how to present them in the most positive way. You may be asked why you are unemployed, why your present salary is low for your age, why your marriage broke up, or why you are applying for a job at less than your present salary. Be sure you have your explanation carefully prepared and memorised.

Common Questions For
Senior Positions

Here are some questions commonly asked by interviewers when the vacancy is senior and involves supervision of staff. In each case, I have given two answers. The puzzle is: some interviewers would prefer the first answer; some would prefer the second!

1. 'Can you take decisions?'

(a) *Sure can. I keep a clean desk. I pride myself on giving decisions on the spot.*

(b) *It depends on the problem. Ninety per cent of the day-to-day issues must be dealt with promptly in the interests of efficiency. But some issues must not be dealt with in haste: such as delicate staff matters, important expenditure decisions, and questions of principle and policy. The skill is to know when to act decisively, and when to seek more information and time for thought. I believe I have that skill.*

2. 'Can you maintain discipline?'

(a) *Yes. I run a tight ship. My staff know I won't stand any nonsense.*

(b) *Discipline is a misleading word. What matters is results: the department must run efficiently, meet its objectives, maintain quality, and conform to policy. With good instructions, training and supervision, that should be possible without the staff feeling an atmosphere of imposed discipline hanging over them. But of course, where someone goes astray she must be brought into line, and I can do that with finality.*

3. 'Can you fire unsatisfactory staff?'

(a) *Yes. It is never pleasant. But I am quite capable of sending someone down the road and I have done it a number of times.*

(b) *In some cases, straightforward dismissal may be necessary: for theft, violence toward other staff, repeated insubordination, and the like. But in general firing is an unwise way of dealing with an unsatisfactory employee. It upsets his friends on the staff. It sends him away badmouthing the organisation and maybe talking to the news media. He may sue for unjustified dismissal. It's far better to persuade him that he is in the wrong job, encourage him to look for another that is more suited to his skills and help him to find such a job.*

The first thing to note is – the interviewer phrased his questions badly. The questions are closed, and therefore could have been answered with *Yes* or *No*. The first applicant did little more than say *Yes*, with a few extra clipped words as embellishment. The second applicant has treated the questions as if they were open, and has given balanced pro-and-con answers, backed up by specifics. His replies are longer, more thoughtful, and contain examples.

A good interviewer would never have asked such closed questions. Instead of asking: 'Can you take decisions?' he would have asked: 'Tell me about the most difficult decision you have had to take in the last year.' Instead of: 'Can you maintain discipline?' he would have said: 'I'd like you to describe an occasion when it was necessary to discipline a member of your staff, and how you went about it.' Instead of: 'Can you fire unsatisfactory staff?' he would have asked: 'What's your preferred method of disengaging an unsatisfactory employee? I'd like some examples.'

Be alert. Where the interviewer frames his questions badly, or asks the wrong question – try to give a good answer nonetheless.

Here are some good, mostly open-ended, questions you ought to be asked when applying for a senior position. They are the sort of questions that establish the fibre (or lack of it) of each applicant. Rehearse your answers – and try to insert such information even where an unskilled interviewer asks other, less revealing questions.

– Tell me what you did yesterday, from the time you arrived at work till the time you went home.

– Roughly, how do you divide your time across your major responsibilities?

– Tell me, with examples, how you take unpopular decisions.

– Tell me how you make those unpopular decisions stick.

– Describe for me a decision you took that everyone else disagreed with.

– Why did they disagree and why did you go ahead anyhow?

– Are you capable of preventing your chief executive, or the board, from doing the wrong thing – in your area of responsibility?

– Give me an example of an occasion when you did just that.

– Do you hire good people?

– What have those people done that proves they are good?

– How often have you altered the structure, or part of the structure, of an organisation?

– What was the effect of altering the structure?

– What methods do you use to ensure deadlines are met?

– How do you assess the productivity of your staff?

– How far ahead do you plan? Please give examples.

– What things do you delegate and what do you refuse to delegate?

– How often do you review your objectives and the methods of achieving them?

– What methods do you use to keep your staff informed?

– What complaints procedures do you provide for your staff?

For senior positions the interviewer will want to know if you can make unpopular decisions, prevent blunders, control difficult situations, establish high standards, contain costs, build profit (or productivity), establish and meet objectives, live half your time in the future, delegate heavily yet keep your finger on pressure points. He or she will want to know if you can choose, train and motivate staff; treat them fairly, resolve their grievances, keep them informed. He or she will want to know how well you accept (and initiate) change, how you handle a crisis, how effective you are at getting the right results, how well you understand policy guidelines and work within them, how well you communicate – with staff and with outsiders.

If you are of the right fibre for a senior position, you won't have any difficulty choosing the right answers to these questions . . . will you?

Your Turn To
Ask Questions

Every good interviewer should provide opportunity for you to ask questions – not only in fairness but also because the quality of your questions will reveal a lot about you. Here's where you round out the information about the firm you gathered in the days before the interview.

First, you need to know about the strength of the company; whether its market share is growing; is it expanding; is it developing new markets; adding new products?

Second, are there any gaps in the job description – to whom would you be responsible; who would be responsible to you; what would be your duties and responsibilities; what would be the limits of your authority; by what factors would your performance be judged?

Third, be clear about the essentials of your conditions of employment: is there a probation period; what is the method of assessing staff performance; what are the grievance procedures; what are the rights and obligations of employees; what are the working hours; what are the redundancy provisions? (These questions need not be asked if the company encloses its printed conditions of employment with its job offer, as it should do – but many do not.)

Fourth, remuneration, Don't try to negotiate a starting salary at this stage, unless the interviewer raises it. But ask about the maximum salary for the position; how frequent are salary reviews; whether reviews include both cost of living adjustments and promotion; is there a bonus scheme?

Fifth, fringe benefits: pension scheme (and level of your contributions), travel or other allowance, life insurance, telephone or other expenses, free car, sick leave and sickness benefits, annual leave, long service leave.

Quite a number of these matters can be left until you find whether you will be made an offer. But at least a selection of them should be covered at the interview.

At the end, when asked whether you have any final question, make it this: 'I am very interested in this position. Have I satisfied you I can do the job well? If not, tell me your doubts and I am sure I can dispel them.'

Of course, there may be a second interview, or an intelligence or aptitude test. You may be asked for samples of your work. References and names of referees will be required if you are being considered for an offer – be ready to provide names of referees additional to those whose written references you included with your application.

Finally, when salary is mentioned, go high. They are indicating that they might want you: find out tactfully how badly they want you. 'This job is an important one; I suggest it is worth more than you are offering for someone of my qualifications. Alternatively, if you would like to put me on trial I would be interested in proving myself worthy of an accelerated rise after six months or a double rise after twelve months.'

If the job is offered to you in the interview, don't accept on the spot. Ask for the offer to be put in writing, and for the company's printed conditions of employment to be enclosed (if they don't have such a document, beware). If the job description was not sent to you before the interview, ask for it to be enclosed with the written offer. It is unwise to decide before you assess those documents.

What's So Special About This Job?

Don't be downcast if you are unsuccessful: analyse what you have learned from the interview and start looking for another job.

Equally, if the job is offered, don't get too excited. Remember, it's your life you are playing with. Just as the interviewer is anxious that he may make the wrong choice – so you should be wary of making a career mistake.

First, what's right with your present job? You know it well; you have built up a work history and therefore job security; you have established pension rights; and if the person above you retires or dies you would be in line for his or her position.

Now what's so good about this job offer: it means more money, and good promotional prospects; new experience; greater challenges; fresh stimulus.

But hang on a minute. Your pension scheme is not transferable, so you would have to start afresh. The new firm's office is further from your home, so travel costs and time wasted would both be greater. There's a probationary period of six months and they *could* decline to confirm your appointment at that time – you'd then be unemployed. And there is that rumour about cutbacks – if they laid off staff, would you be the first to go, on the 'last on, first off' principle? And what was that bit about unpaid over-time? Come to think of it, the written conditions of employment are pretty skimpy – light on employee rights and heavy on obligations.

Yes, there are gains and prospects. But do the advantages out-weigh the risks? Of course, it would be nice to get away from that picky boss you have now – but the new one sounded a bit autocratic at the interview. Maybe no boss is perfect? Perhaps your present boss is not that bad after all. For one thing, he does seem to give appreciation when it counts – at salary review time.

And there is the new work you will be doing – maybe it won't suit you. If you end up unhappy, and look again for a fresh job, you may wish your springboard was your present position rather than this one you're toying with.

Remember: there's a sea of jobs out there and you can cast your net as frequently as you like. You have been offered this job – but if you had been offered two at the same time, is this the one you would have taken? The fact you have landed this offer probably means you can land another.

So how do you decide? There's only one way to make up your mind: ensure you have a full written job description and written conditions of employment. Ask questions about the stability of the new firm. Then take a large sheet of paper and write down all the pluses and minuses in two columns. Take a few days to think about it all. Then decide. And good luck.

Develop Your Skill With Words

Skill with words is essential to the career advancement of most people. You may be asked to chair a meeting, address a group of clients, brief your boss, appear before the board, be interviewed on TV, put a case to a government agency, outline a proposal you have thought up, farewell an employee, give a staff training talk, write a report, prepare an advertising proposal, assess a new development project, explain a budget over-run.

Other chapters in this book will help you with these tasks: how to analyse a situation; see other points of view; research the subject; structure a case; and present it in clear, logical, persuasive fashion.

In this chapter, too, we have discussed how to plan for any exercise in communication; how to anticipate what others will do and say; how to construct and rehearse your own case; how to present that case well.

I am impressed constantly by the way the various skills of communication interlock and reinforce each other: the skills of debating, of impromptu speaking, of good command of language, of chairmanship, of dealing with the news media, of persuasion, of humorous speech, of social speaking. What a shame it is that some people regard themselves as writers only, others as speakers only; that some like machines but not books; that some understand figures but think themselves hopeless with words. And that so many good people blunder into the interview room, thrash about in acute discomfort for forty minutes, then depart in frustrated knowledge that the job they so wanted will not be theirs.

It need not be so.

Summary

1. Read widely about interview techniques; build your skills by applying for jobs.

2. Plan your responses to the most likely questions; memorise your qualifications, experience and skills.

3. Beware of bad first impressions.

4. Understand the three main types of interview.

5. Watch for open and closed questions and know how to respond.

6. If silence is used as a tactic, don't be drawn into unwise disclosures.

7. Rehearse your answers to those often-asked questions.

8. Plan positively worded responses to questions about blots on your record and deficiencies in your experience.

9. The questions you ask are important.

10. If offered the job, consider carefully the pluses and minuses.

11. Always be aware of the ways in which your skill with words can boost your career.

Chapter Nine

WHAT MAKES A REALLY
GOOD CHAIRPERSON?

Guestimates are never to be encouraged, but here is one I feel impel-
led to make: 90 per cent of all meetings are too long, badly structured, boring in some parts, indecisive in others, and a waste of
much of the talent present.

Why? The fault lies usually with the chairperson. Of course,
some of those who attend may be difficult, obtuse, bloody-minded,
obstructive. But a good chairperson will cope. More than that, he
or she will outwit the spoilers with good humour, firm control of
procedure, and a clear grasp of the essentials of debate.

In this chapter we will discuss: preparatory work; the art of draft-
ing an agenda; the conventions on motions and amendments; what
'formal motions' mean; coping with rebellion; and the knack of
suppressing the long-winded and encouraging the meek.

Broadly, there are two main types of meeting:

The one-off meeting. This is held for a particular purpose: a discussion on a community problem; a conference or seminar; a social
gathering; a political meeting; and so on. Thus there is no prior history of minutes, resolutions, policies, and so on. Often there are no
decisions to be made – the chairperson's task is merely to welcome
people, introduce people, thank people.

The regular meeting. Here there is a body of precedent to guide the
chairperson, who probably will be well-known to everyone present
and steeped in knowledge of the organisation from years of service.

In Chapter 7 we discussed some of the skills of people who chair
(or M.C.) one-off meetings. Here we will concentrate upon the requirements of regular meetings, which range from sports or cul-
tural clubs, to boards of business firms, to public service bodies, and
so on.

The most skilful chairman only *seems* to be impartial and democratic. Much of the time, when the issue is of no great moment, he

will bend readily to the collective wish. But on some matters he will seek to achieve a specific decision because he is alert to under-currents among the membership and to attempts of some participants to outwit the remainder.

While in theory the chairman is 'the servant of the meeting', he has an obligation to see that decisions are arrived at in orderly fashion; that they are derived logically from sound evidence; that the meeting is not bulldozed into a resolution it will later regret. Especially, he must ensure that a vocal, strong-willed person does not force the meeting into unwilling acceptance of a minority viewpoint.

In the most difficult situation a chairman must keep the peace among two or more warring factions. To be relaxed, easygoing and impartial in such situations invites disaster. The chairman must be well-prepared, constantly aware of competing undercurrents, and always two jumps ahead of everyone else.

The Ideal Chairperson:
Impartial, Democratic, And
Highly Manipulative!

Obviously, a chairperson rules only because sufficient people have respect for his or her authority. To retain their confidence he or she must be (or seem to be) fair, objective, impartial, democratic, sensitive to the collective wish of the meeting, and free of any compulsion to impose his or her own views.

That of course assumes everyone else will be equally fair-minded! But some will be motivated by passionate beliefs, half-baked ideas, inaccurate information, intense dislike of other members, jealousies, ambitions, insecurities, poor remembrance of past decisions. Some of the more strong-willed participants may be intent on out-manoeuvring opponents to achieve their own ends. Thus an over democratic chairman may find himself out-flanked, bewildered and without effective control.

The Delicate Art of
Preparing An Agenda

Every meeting should have an agenda, preferably thought out at leisure, carefully structured, supported where necessary with background papers and recommendations. Ideally it should be circulated well in advance. Otherwise, how will people know what will be dealt with, and how can they collect their thoughts so as to be most useful?

If the chairwoman does not prepare the agenda, she should discuss it fully with the compiler a day or so beforehand to be familiar with all issues and with options available.

Many meetings have brief, straightforward agendas, something like this:

Apologies for absence
Minutes of previous meeting
Matters arising from the minutes
Correspondence
Matters arising from the correspondence
Reports of sub-committees
Matters arising from the reports
Several major items each deserving a separate listing (e.g. annual ball; visit by overseas touring team)
Late matters
Financial statement
General business
Date of next meeting

But other agendas are rather more complex. Specific policy issues, controversial events, delicate staff matters, legal wrangles, ethical dilemmas become separate agenda items, often supported by complex background papers.

In what order should these items be listed? As a guide, consider the first rule of agenda making: *people always linger over early items and speed up on the tail-end items*. So weightier matters should go up front, while routine items of information and trivial items requiring automatic approval should be clustered at the end.

Some chairmen or chairwomen abuse this rule, by putting a controversial item at the back of the agenda, hoping the participants will be ready to dispose of it quickly when all are weary and ready to go home. This device can succeed superbly, but it will become obvious and build resentment if used often.

Another subterfuge used to control quarrelsome factions is crowding the agenda. Then the chairperson will seek to traverse controversial issues at speed, on the ground that there is a heavy load of business. This clumsy device seldom works, and can provoke much resistance.

A better way to prevent a touchy item from polarising the meeting is to make use of the second rule of agenda making: *people cannot easily switch from laughter to anger*. So put the tender issue in the middle of the agenda (by which time some of the early loquaciousness will have waned) and try to precede it with one or more lighthearted or good-humoured items. If you can crack jokes, commend people, report on a great success, and *then* go into the contentious issue, you will find it easier to keep temperatures down.

Of course, an adroit chairperson will never rely on structure of the agenda alone to prevent or minimise conflict. He or she will telephone in advance a member who has strong views on the touchy subject: 'At the next meeting, Jack, our lawyer will propose that we sue Snatch and Grab Ltd for breach of copyright of our name. I know we are all upset at the misuse of our name, but a lawsuit would be expensive and might well fail. Since you have a lot of experience in the organisation I thought it would be very helpful to get your opinion. Is there some less expensive way to get Snatch and Grab to back off?'

When Jack responds vehemently that the thieves must be sued regardless of cost, the chairman remains non-committal. He has the information he needs – Jack will express himself uncompromisingly at the meeting. Next, the chairperson phones a moderate, finds she is averse to a lawsuit, and says, 'Thank you, Marion. You have helped clarify my thinking. I hope you will speak to this matter on Wednesday.' Having ensured there will be a balance of opinion expressed, he or she will feel more confident of obtaining a sound decision.

Sometimes, on a really momentous issue, a chairperson will take advance soundings of most or all committee members.

The Pre-Meeting Checks Of
The Watchful Chairperson

Be sure you re-read the minutes of the last two or three meetings for: (a) items deferred to this meeting, (b) persons delegated tasks for this meeting, (c) sub-committees due to report. Make sure everyone is reminded of their obligations and of the date by which any written report is required.

Every chairperson must know (or rekindle his memory of) the rules. These include:

1. Any law of the land that governs your type of organisation, including those that lay down requirements for declaration of potentially conflicting interests.

2. The common law decisions of the courts that have revolved around points of meeting procedure.

3. The constitution of your organisation (if it has one). This can be known by a variety of names: the aims and objects; the charter; the terms of reference; the articles (or memorandum) of association; the bylaws; the rules.

4. The 'standing orders' (if any) of your organisation, which will set out in some detail how meetings are to be run.

5. Previous resolutions of the organisation, as found in past minutes. Plus rulings of past chairmen or chairwomen; any written procedures that have become accepted; also, customs of other similar organisations may be copied where there is no other guide.

If there is a 'policy book' listing all past decisions, know it thoroughly. If not, compile one of your own. The purpose of this document is not to prevent a change of policy; but to ensure such a change is made knowingly, and by rescinding the previous resolution.

Before each meeting the chairperson must ensure sufficient notice is given (to *all* participants). The period of notice may be specified in the rules, and ideally the agenda should be sent out with the notice of meeting.

Getting a Quorum

At any gathering where the rules specify that a quorum must be present, the chairperson must ensure sufficient numbers have gathered before the proceedings are opened. If there is no quorum, the start of the meeting can be delayed, or absentees who live nearby telephoned. In desperation some ill-attended meetings go ahead with a telephone line open to a member who could not attend, or the meeting will take *pro forma* decisions and have them ratified later by other members. Such devices are ill-advised, and decisions so taken would probably be declared invalid if challenged in court. If you do not have a quorum, do not allow the meeting to begin. And if you lose the quorum when some members depart early, bring the meeting to a close.

The presence of observers, or people 'in attendance', may be confusing. They should not be counted as part of the quorum. Further, you will need to be sure whether the rules permit observers to take part in the discussion. Even if they can, be sure an observer does not move or second any motion. Nor should an observer be allowed to shape the discussions so that he or she becomes the *de facto* mover of the motion.

Open the meeting at the advertised time, not before, or you may be challenged by someone who arrives at the due hour and misses some of the proceedings.

Ensure everyone is seated, then with a smile and in a conversational tone, say warmly: 'Welcome everyone. I declare the meeting open.' It is from this point that the minutes begin; anything said before the meeting is opened should not be recorded. Similarly, at the end of the proceedings the chairperson should declare the meeting closed (or adjourned), for that makes plain where the record ends.

If the agenda has not been circulated in advance it is essential that the chairperson read it through at the outset, preferably distributing copies.

Even where it has been circulated, spend some time on it. Ask first when people have to leave the meeting. You may find you have three hours. Suggest to the members that you want to get through a certain number of items in each of the three hours. When they agree, you will be well placed to hurry them along if later they lag behind schedule.

Running a Smooth Meeting

Modes of address should be consistently formal or consistently informal. A man in the chair is addressed as Mr Chairman or Mr Chairperson; a woman as Madame Chairman, Madame Chairperson, Madam Chair or Madam-in-the-Chair (she should choose how she wishes to be addressed). Participants in a formal meeting, or where they are unfamiliar with each other, may be addressed as Mr Blenkinsop or Miss Thimblefoot. But where possible they should address each other by their first names.

Unless the rules constrain you, as chairperson you will have to decide how strictly you will run your meetings. Will you insist that each person may speak only once on each issue? Or will you be more relaxed, even dispense with formal motions, allowing people to speak freely, pulling them back when they stray from the point, summing up at the appropriate moment, then asking: 'Am I correct that we all agree this is what we want to do?'

One way to keep things on the rails is to require everyone to 'speak through the chair'. This means Alfred Grumblechops cannot address Muriel Shrillspeak directly ('Muriel, you're off your head . . .') but must say "Mr Chairman, I disagree with Muriel's comment . . .' In this way, tempers are kept down and the chairman can more easily intervene.

How should you develop a good atmosphere? Remember the rules on presentation: eye contact, pausation, a genial expression. Don't concentrate your gaze on one person; let your eyes rove over the circle of faces. Never hurry. Be deliberate. Don't be afraid to allow long pauses to develop while you study your papers, or ruminate upon something said. A chairperson who speaks quickly and is always in a rush unsettles his or her members.

Use friendly language, a dash of humour, encouragement and sympathy. Take special care with those who are shy or inarticulate. It's a good idea to warn such a person in advance that you will call on her to speak to a particular item on the agenda; this lets her get her thoughts straight at leisure.

Each item on the agenda will be introduced by the chairperson, or he or she will call upon someone else to do so. Ideally, there should be a background paper, otherwise people are faced with a brief and inadequate phrase (say, 'Increase in rental charges'). The background paper should always begin with a recommendation, which if agreed with may become the motion ('That we reject the proposed increase in rent and seek an independent valuer's report on what is a fair rental for our premises').

You may begin discussion on an item thus: 'There is a paper before us which sets out various options and makes a recommendation. Does anyone wish to speak for or against the recommendation?'

If it seems quite soon that everyone is in favour of the recommendation, you can sum up quickly: 'Do I have the feeling of the meeting that we all agree with the recommendation . . .? If so will someone move that it be adopted . . . thank you . . . and do we have a seconder?'

These are good words: 'Is it the wish of the meeting . . .?' Or: 'We seem to be agreed that . . .' Or: 'Do I understand correctly that we all think . . .?' The chairperson who speaks thus cannot be accused of forcing his or her own views on the meeting – and can easily pull back if the presumption proves incorrect.

Where discussion pitches inconclusively back and forth, the chairperson should intervene to draw together the threads of the debate: 'I suggest the issue has been narrowed down to these two alternatives . . . if so, I wonder if we can look more closely at the advantages and disadvantages of each . . .'

The single most important skill is to be able to 'read' the progress of a debate and to isolate the essential ingredients: 'Can I summarise the main points raised so far . . .?' Then he or she will help the meeting discard the poorer options by referring to valid objections raised in discussion. Thus the members will be nudged tactfully towards a decision.

What do you do when someone makes a really daft statement? Often, nothing. Just let the statement hang in the air, and wait for another comment to carry the discussion forward. Or simply say, 'Thank you for that comment, Henry. Does anyone else wish to say anything?' It is important that the chairperson should not 'put people down'. If a member stubbornly pursues an impracticable idea, just pause, and say doubtfully: 'Well-l-l-l . . .' and someone else will chime in with reasons why the proposal cannot be entertained. A good chairperson will use sparingly his or her power to smother ideas. The skill is to recognise harebrained or dangerous proposals and try to isolate them, so that they do not gain momentum.

Some meetings are very informal. A matter will be discussed, the chairperson will sum up, everyone will murmur agreement, and the minutes will eventually record: 'The meeting decided that a ratcatcher be employed to rid the front office of its unwelcome visitor.' No motions, no amendments, no foreshadowings, no points of order. Just relaxed consensus and an easy run for the chairman.

Except that next meeting a grim battle erupts over the accuracy of the minutes: as to just what was decided and whether a majority was in agreement!

To prevent such disputes a number of rules of meeting procedure have grown up and are recognised in many countries.

As mentioned earlier, some are found either in the law or else in the constitution, rules or practices of your organisation. Apart from such restraints, most meetings may 'regulate their own procedure'. Nonetheless, they are expected to follow certain generally accepted conventions – which are discussed in the rest of this chapter.

Motions, Resolutions
And Amendments

A *motion* is simply a proposal that the meeting should take a particular decision. Some chairmen insist that nothing may be discussed unless there is a motion before the meeting. This is a rigid requirement which can lead to endless amendments as it becomes clear that the original motion was woefully inadequate. It can be much better to allow some discussion, then say to a speaker: 'Do you have a motion to propose?'

Note that a motion and a *resolution* are not the same, though people wrongly use them interchangeably. A resolution is a motion that has been carried (agreed by a majority of those present). The correct usage is to refer to 'the resolution that was passed at the last meeting', not to 'the motion that was passed . . .' Similarly, you should refer to 'the motion that was defeated at the last meeting', not 'the resolution that was defeated'.

A good motion will begin with the word 'That'; will be precise and unambiguous; will not contravene any rules; and will be phrased positively, not negatively.

The chairperson may *rule a motion out of order* if it is ambiguous; redundant; phrased in offensive language; goes outside the scope of the organisation's activities; breaches or contradicts the organisation's constitution; or is unlawful. If the motion contradicts a past decision, he or she will warn the members to rescind the earlier decision first (but if a new decision inadvertently contradicts an earlier one, the new decision over-rides the other).

When a motion is proposed, and the chairperson has no objection to it, he or she will ask if there is a seconder – unless someone has already leapt in with 'Mr Chairman, I second the motion.' It is generally accepted that if no-one is prepared to second it the motion *lapses for want of a seconder*. Clearly there is not enough support to warrant taking up any more time of the meeting.

Always, the mover has the right to speak first to his motion. Some authorities say this may be done before it is seconded; others say it must be done after. Unless the rules of your organisation are specific, it is for you to decide. The seconder has the right (if he wishes) to speak next, but may *reserve the right* to speak later; thus he can see if there is any opposition to the motion, then come in with a statement of support plus answers to objections raised. Sometimes a person will be unsure whether he supports the motion, yet wish to hear more; so he will say 'Madame Chairperson, I *second the motion pro forma*'. A motion that might otherwise lapse thus receives further consideration.

When mover and seconder have been offered their right to speak, the chairperson then opens the discussion to the others, and should take them in the order they catch his eye. It is good practice to say: 'I will take Tabitha first, followed by Cadwallader, then Louisa.'

The chairperson must prevent people straying from the point, repeating themselves, covering the same ground as earlier speakers, reminiscing, or otherwise wasting time. Where several have spoken in favour of the motion, ask if anyone wishes to speak against it and take him next, so that he is not put off by weight of favourable opinion. Where clearly no-one wishes to put a contrary view, you should put the motion straight to the vote.

Where there is strong difference of opinion, some speaking for the motion and some against, one or more of those who have already spoken may seek to have a second go. If the rules of the organisation prevent *second speeches,* the chairperson must comply. If not, he should decide (at his first meeting) whether he will allow them. I favour permitting them, for time and again I have seen a potentially bad decision turn into quite the right one when a person, with his second speech, seized upon the nub of the issue which had escaped everyone else. Whatever rule is applied on second speeches, convention allows the mover of the motion a *right of reply* at the end of any debate where opposition to his proposal has been expressed.

During discussion a member of the group may decide that he is in favour of the motion but the wording is not quite right, so he proposes an *amendment*. An amendment must not contradict the main motion (otherwise it is not an amendment but an attempt to defeat the main motion). It may add, delete or substitute words, phrases or even whole sentences. It should have a seconder, and the procedure is the same as for a motion.

If an amendment is carried, it becomes part of the motion. The amended motion is then still open for discussion, and further amendments may be proposed and passed. From time to time the air may be thick with amendments – what should the chairman do? I suggest you allow only one motion or one amendment to be dealt with at any time. Those chairmen who permit amendments to amendments risk unholy confusion. Nonetheless, a person who thinks an amendment unsatisfactory can, when speaking against it, imply a better one. Moreover, she is entitled to *foreshadow:* 'Mr Chairman, I think Bernice's amendment is unwise and I want to foreshadow a different amendment I wish to move later.' She will then give the wording of the amendment she has in mind. In this way she seeks to show a better wording is possible, and to influence people to vote against Bernice's amendment. Motions can be fore-shadowed too, and often a mover will ask permission to withdraw a motion or an amendment when a better option is presented. *If all those present agree,* the chairperson may accept such withdrawal.

To sum up:

1. Once a motion has been proposed, it must be seconded and discussed before being put to the vote.

2. Where there is one amendment, it must be seconded and discussed, then put to the vote. If carried, it becomes part of the motion. Then the amended motion itself must be discussed and voted upon.

3. Where there is more than one amendment, each amendment should be seconded, discussed and voted upon *separately*. Then the motion, as finally amended, should be discussed and voted upon.

Before voting takes place the chairperson should ensure that the motion or amendment (or amended motion) is read out – even written on a blackboard. Often a chairperson will ask a mover to write down his or her motion or amendment and have it passed to the chair.

Voting is commonly done by a voice call ('All those in favour say Aye . . . All those against, No . . . the motion is carried'). If there is doubt, the chairperson will call for a show of hands, or even a ballot. Often the rules will specify which system is to be used; they may also state that the chairperson has a *casting vote,* which is an extra vote to be used in the event of a tie. By tradition the chairman casts his vote for the status quo – thus ensuring that any radical new proposal must obtain an absolute majority before succeeding.

Finally, any member may give *notice of motion,* which allows everyone to think about a matter in advance. Notice may be given at the start of a meeting that a motion will be moved later under general business; or may be given during one meeting that a motion will be moved at the next; or may be given between meetings by writing to the secretary who will circulate the motion before the next meeting.

Procedural Rules That Help
Keep The Meeting Flowing

Any motion calling for an action, or a statement of principle, from the group is known as a *substantive* motion. Any motion referring to the way the meeting is conducted is a *procedural* motion. Common procedural motions are:

1. *That the question be now put.* The intention is to halt time-wasting discussion and have the issue put to a vote. If not carried, discussion will continue.

2. *That the question be NOT now put.* This is aimed at preventing a vote being taken on the issue. If carried, the substantive motion cannot be voted upon at that meeting; if lost, the substantive motion must be put to the vote immediately.

3. *That we proceed to the next business.* Similar in intent to 2. above. If carried, discussion is postponed.

4. *That the debate be adjourned.* Similar to 2. and 3. except that it often expresses intention to resume at a particular time, perhaps after further information has been obtained, or when an absent member of the group will be able to take part or be questioned. A variation of this tactic is to move that the *meeting* itself be adjourned.

Other procedural motions that try to move a meeting on by postponing or abandoning discussion on a substantive motion are: 'That the meeting postpone consideration of the subject'; 'That the question lie on the table', 'That the recommendation be referred back to the committee.'

Unfortunately, the conventions surrounding these procedural motions are very complex. Some may be refused by the chairman, others not; on some discussion may be permitted, on others not; plus many more stipulations. The full guide to procedural motions is given in a number of reference works, such as *How to Run a Meeting* by C. F. Bentley (Coles, Toronto) or *Guide for Meetings and Organisations* by N. E. Renton (Hicks Smith, Sydney).

Few chairmen or chairwomen can learn all these rules by heart. Find out what each of the motions means and, if faced with it, deal firmly with it in the most commonsense way. In particular, be ready to reject a closure motion where you feel the subject has been insufficiently discussed. Remember this old saying: it is better for a chairperson to give a wrong decision with confidence, than to waver in confusion.

There is one situation where rules are set aside: when the meeting decides to go *into committee* (also known as 'the committee of the whole'). This has two purposes: to allow free debate without formal rules; and to prevent the discussion being reported by any journalist present. The first purpose is unnecessary if you do not apply formal rules; the relaxed, informal meeting is already 'in committee' because it allows free debate – and can easily exclude journalists by moving that the proceedings on any issue are not for publication.

The Many Devices
For Keeping Order

Sometimes a chairperson will fail to notice a breach of the rules – or may commit one himself. Any member may then raise a *point of order,* grounds for which include: that the meeting lacks a quorum; that a speaker is using unacceptable language or personal abuse; that a speaker has strayed from the point; that a motion goes beyond the organisation's terms of reference, or breaches its rules.

When you hear 'Point of order, Madame Chairwoman' you should halt the speaker and, if he is standing, ask him to resume his seat. Then ask the interrupter to 'speak to' (i.e. give grounds for) his point of order. You may also allow the person interrupted to 'respond to' (i.e. refute) the challenge. But allow only the briefest of speeches from each; then give a crisp, clear ruling; and straightaway invite the interrupted speaker to resume. Don't become flustered; if unsure what to do, toss a mental coin and announce: 'I uphold the point of order', or 'I disallow the point of order'. Don't dither: if unsure, bluff it out!

While a point of order may interrupt a speaker, a *point of misrepresentation* may be taken only when he has finished. This occurs when a previous speaker objects that his remarks have been distorted, taken out of context or otherwise misrepresented.

The third 'point' to be aware of is the *point of information*. This occurs at the end of a speech where another participant says: 'Point of information, Mr Chairman. May I ask Alphonse whether the average income figures he quoted are median averages?' Such questions must be brief, the speaker's answer is usually accepted, and normally there is no discussion.

To keep order the chairperson commonly requires nothing more than force of character, coolness, and ability to give firm, fair rulings. But if 'toughing it out' fails there are several other devices at your disposal. You may *reprimand* a member who is persistently discourteous, abusive or defiant. You may *prohibit* a vexatious member from speaking or voting for a period; you may demand an *apology* on pain of expulsion; you may *exclude* from the meeting anyone who violently disrupts the proceedings. But you had better gauge well the feeling of the participants before taking drastic action against one of their number. Sometimes the best action is to adjourn the meeting to a specified date. That allows tempers to cool and provides time for reflection.

But what if the chairperson is the offender?

1. A member may say: 'I move that the meeting *disagree with the chairwoman's ruling.*' She must then leave the chair (no seconder is needed), to be replaced by the deputy chairperson or some other nominated person. Both she and the challenger may speak to the motion, which is then altered to read 'That the chairwoman's ruling be upheld' before voting occurs. Whether or not the challenge is upheld, the chairwoman returns to the chair. If the challenge *is* upheld, she simply reverses her decision and the meeting continues; such a reversal is not serious and should be taken in stride.

2. If the chairperson is *censured* by the meeting that is indeed serious. This may be because of abusive language, because he is drunk, or because he is acting in a dictatorial, unfair or prejudiced manner. Though censure is no reason for resignation, it is a warning that the members have been seriously put out by the person they chose to be their chairman.

3. A motion of *no-confidence* is worst of all. In one form it reads: 'That the meeting no longer has confidence in the chairman', and if carried removes him from the chair for the rest of the meeting, which continues with another chairman. The more severe form of this motion reads: 'That Mr Jones no longer enjoys the confidence of the organisation.' If carried it removes him from office – though he may stand for the resulting vacancy.

A tactful alternative to disciplining a wayward chairperson is to move that the meeting adjourn to a later date. In the interval the chairperson will have time to think about his or her behaviour and some influential members may 'have a chat' with him or her. In this way a basically sound chairperson may be rehabilitated.

Summary

The ideal chairperson shows these qualities:

1. The strength of character to take command, and to maintain discipline in a firm, impartial way.

2. The ability to 'read' the progress of a discussion and to sum up succinctly; to set a brisk pace; to foster a good-humoured atmosphere; to build a sense of collaboration.

3. The gift of making everyone feel useful, of encouraging the faint-hearted and subduing the vociferous.

4. The insight to know the participants, their prejudices, pet causes, jealousies and machinations; and to ensure that despite conflicting ambitions everyone will receive a fair hearing.

5. The tenacity to learn the rules and history of the organisation, and to do adequate preparation for each meeting.

6 The humility to submerge his or her views while sifting those of the participants to arrive at the common good.

Chapter Ten

HOW TO HANDLE A PRESS
OR TV INTERVIEW

There is a common belief that journalists feed off tragedy, human misery and innocent error. They are thought to be driven by a compulsion to scoop their fellows, if only by hours or even minutes. They are seen as interested primarily in getting a story, not in pursuing the truth. They appear not to mind if they report an inaccuracy, for that means tomorrow they will be able to feature a hot denial from someone else. They are said to foment discord, by prompting one person to be provocative, and later reaping an easy follow-up story from an irate opponent.

How widespread is this cynical view of the media? In 1983 a nationwide poll showed that only 13.7 per cent of Americans had 'a great deal of confidence in the press'. In the same year, another survey showed that only 11 per cent of Australians rated journalists 'very high' or 'high' for ethics and honesty. Through much of the free world (and doubtless it is one price of freedom) the media is accused of sensationalism, distortion, bias, self-indulgence and a warped sense of the public interest. Journalists are felt to be rude, arrogant, insensitive, intrusive and often ghoulish.

Like all generalisations, this view of the media is unfair. As in any profession, there are good and bad practitioners. The best journalists are people of unswerving integrity, who do weigh the consequences of their actions before plunging into print or onto tape or film. They check their facts with care, and are prepared to forgo a scoop in order to ensure balance and accuracy.

Nonetheless, dealing with the media is a lottery. The journalist who interviews you may be reliable or unreliable, experienced or inexperienced, open-minded or prejudiced. Especially if he works for an unblushingly sensational editor or producer, you can expect him to try to force your comments into the mould of his preconstructed story.

Are journalists entitled to complaints of their own about the people they inverview? Often, yes. Too many people make incautious statements, then try to slide out of embarrassment by claiming they were misquoted. Too often, they do not prepare adequately for the interview; neglect to add balancing statements to what they say; draw sweeping conclusions from too few examples; rely on what someone has told them; fail to check their facts before expounding them.

When an inexperienced journalist meets an inept interviewee, disaster is likely: the faults of the one will compound those of the other.

With luck, a poor interview will do you little harm. Though you may feel uneasy that you have been wrongly or selectively quoted, the overall impression may be one that you can live with. But when the interview goes wrong, really wrong, it can alter your life. You may be made a figure of ridicule; become embroiled in a protracted dispute you never wanted; even have your job put at risk.

So I have prepared this defence kit against the media, which in part is a defence kit against yourself. In this chapter we will discuss the hazards of the telephone interview; how to handle yourself in front of the television camera; the special requirements of radio; dealing with a press reporter; how to recognise trap questions; ways of reducing the chances of being misreported; how to tell whether an interview is likely to be abrasive.

Whether you encounter journalists rarely, or routinely, you need to know something about dealing with them. As you progress in your career, you will probably be asked more often to handle publicity, or to respond to a request for an interview. In some organisations publicity is so essential it is built into the work-plan; getting a weekly or even daily headline becomes a requirement of the marketing strategy.

If you bring to an interview nothing but naiveté and nervous trust in the journalist, you are vulnerable. Should she be intent on investigating you or your company for presumed failings, the contest will be unequal. An experienced interviewer is master of the situation; is sole judge of which of your statements he will use; is adept at drawing unwise admissions from callow subjects; and can interleave your comments with others in a way that is outside your control. It is the purpose of this chapter to redress the balance; by building up your knowledge of what to expect and how to react.

Must You Agree To
Be Interviewed?

Of course not. You may decline, and need not give a reason. Most often, the invitation will be by telephone. Let the journalist do the talking – outlining the matters on which she would like to question you. Don't volunteer anything. If you simply listen, she will probably keep talking, telling you broadly what she has in mind. Prompt her occasionally: 'What else do you intend to cover?'

If you feel you cannot contribute usefully, or that you may get out of your depth, decline politely. She may persist, in which case it is best to deflect her: 'I'm afraid I can't help. But I suggest you try either the Master Builders' Association or the Building Research Institute.' Some reporters will not let go, prodding you to take part and suggesting that if you do not participate the story will be unbalanced. Too bad: if she ends up with something lopsided, that's her problem, not yours.

What if the reporter says she will do the story anyway – and hints that you may not come out of it well unless your side is heard? Here you have to weigh up costs and benefits. If you take part, you may be able to reduce or smother criticism. But if you feel it is a no-win situation, stay away. Especially if the matter has been raised already in the media; and your reputation has already been damaged; and further publicity is likely to increase the damage – then remain politely resolute.

Is there any way you can tell, during the initial approach, that an abrasive interview is likely? Yes. If the journalist is guarded in her explanation of what she wants to talk about; if she fends off your questions about the subject matter; if her voice is cagey – then you should be wary. The more open a journalist is, the more freely she reveals the line she intends to pursue, the more reassured you can feel.

Convention has it that while interviewers are obliged to tell you the broad subject areas they wish to cover, they are not obliged to tell you the particular questions they will use. To hell with convention. Be inquisitive: 'What sort of questions do you have in mind?' Often you will be told some at least. So probe politely and persistently, trying all the time to gauge from her degree of reticence what she intends.

Those Tricky Telephone
Interviews

You are at a disadvantage in dealing with a disembodied voice. There is little time to gather your thoughts, and you cannot tell which of your comments the reporter is writing down. To see how easy it is to be bustled into unwise statements, let's look at the tangle that ace fullback, Martin Wingfoot, gets himself into when he answers the phone:

'This is Albert Inkblot of the Times,*' he hears an unfamiliar voice say. 'I understand all the players in your team are upset about the new training schedule Coach Blair has laid down.'*

'Um — yes,' Wingfoot says hesitantly. 'Yes, we're worried that the exercises we are being put through may cause injuries.'

'How does it affect you?'

'Well . . . I've got this bad back, from a motorbike accident a few years ago, and some of the exercises put a lot of strain on it.'

Inkblot gives him no time to reflect: 'Could the training programme cause you permanent injury?'

'I'm not sure. I suppose it's possible.'

By now Inkblot is riding hard on his prepared theme: 'Are you angry with Coach Blair for forcing these exercises on you and risking permanent injury to his star fullback?'

'Well . . . I am a bit upset.'

'Do you think your coach is so intent on victory that he's prepared to risk the health of his players?'

'Well, he certainly is hell-bent on winning the Shield. But then we all are.'

'Could this training schedule lead to a trail of injuries for the team?'

'I don't know. But we are worried about it.'

And so it goes on. Then next day there it all is in the *Times:*

STAR FULLBACK SLAMS COACH; HELL-BENT ON WINNING SHIELD; DOESN'T CARE ABOUT HIS PLAYERS

Yesterday Martin Wingfoot, ace fullback of the Havering Rangers, revealed that Coach Blair is forcing his players into training schedules that could cause permanent injury.

'He is hell-bent on winning the Shield,' said Martin. 'There could be a trail of injuries along the way.'

We can see what went wrong. Wingfoot weakly allowed the reporter to dominate the interview, to use leading questions and pursue a prepared line without interruption. Wingfoot did not realise the carefully rehearsed questions were loaded, with answers and attitudes built into them: 'Are you angry with Coach Blair . . .?' 'Could this training schedule lead to a trail of injuries . . .?' In part, Wingfoot allowed himself to be prompted and manipulated so that his answers fitted Inkblot's preconceived theme; and in part he did not realise that if he failed to specifically disagree with emotive terms used by Inkblot, it would be assumed he agreed with them.

Above all, Wingfoot failed to take control. Had he insisted on jotting down Inkblot's questions, without comment, then he might have given a very different response two hours later, after due reflection and maybe telephone calls to other players. He might then have stated plainly to Inkblot that Coach Blair is a fine tactician who has the full support of the team; nonetheless his new training schedules may be too tough for some players, especially those with weaknesses from previous injuries; so the players intend discussing the matter with Coach Blair and expect him to be very sympathetic. Having said all that over the phone, he would have asked Inkblot to read it back to him.

It would then be difficult for Inkblot to manufacture a controversy.

Insist On Time
To Prepare

When you discover it's a journalist on the phone, take immediate control of your tongue. Pick up paper and pen – asking him to wait if necessary while you do so – then write down his name and the newspaper, magazine, TV or radio station he represents. Next, jot down the reason for his call. Volunteer absolutely no information, but ask him to slow down, or repeat himself, until you are quite sure you have the essence of what he wants to question you about.

It is at this point you will decline to comment if you decide not to become involved.

If you are prepared to take part, decide whether you need time to gather information, consult your files, talk to your boss or to colleagues. It is best if the journalist can come to you. In a face-to-face situation you have more control: you can watch him write down your answers; you can slow down if you are going too fast; and if you see him stop writing when you add a qualification to one of your statements, you can insist he writes down the qualification too.

Often, especially where he is calling from out of town, the journalist will have to conduct the interview by phone. So decide whether you need time to think matters over – and ask him to call back in (say) an hour. Only where you are very familiar with the subject should you comment immediately.

Some telephone interviews are loaded with risk. For example, where a reporter asks you for a comment on a new development: 'This morning the Loan Sharks and Usurers Association said lending rates will have to rise substantially. The *Times* would very much like your comment on that.' You haven't seen the statement; you don't know whether the reporter is citing it accurately, or whether he is picking sentences out of context, or the reasons behind the statement. Your best response is: 'I cannot comment unless I see the statement. Can someone bring a copy of it round to me?'

If the caller is from out of town, ask whether he has the statement in front of him; then ask for it to be read to you slowly, and write down at least the essence of it. Then decide whether you need time to respond – in which case he will have to call you back.

During your preparation time you should do four things:

(a) Sort out what you *can* say.

(b) Sort out what you can *not* go into.

(c) Organise your material into a sequence.

(d) Make your statement concise and colourful – and be sure you can support all of it with satisfactory evidence.

Make jottings of this material on a sheet of paper. If giving the information on the phone, tick off each item as you read it out – then ask for the statement to be read back to you as a check. If doing a face-to-face press interview, again tick off your material as you give it – and make notes afterward of any additional things you have said. Sometimes you may use a tape recorder – and indeed the journalist may use one too.

How To Deal With
The Print Media

Remember this: never expect a print journalist to present your views exactly as you would. She brings her own point of view to the story; she selects, rearranges, condenses and often weaves in the views of others. Some of your comments will be quoted directly; others will be given in reported speech. She may quote the first half of one of your sentences and abandon the second half. Most disconcerting of all, a minor passing comment of yours, made casually and almost in throwaway fashion, may be lifted out and given prominence in headline and introductory paragraph.

Moreover, though the reporter approached you and pressed you for comment, her story may give the opposite impression – that you initiated the whole thing and were only too eager to burst into print. Thus after reluctantly agreeing to be interviewed, and having mildly disagreed with comments the reporter says the mayor made to her that morning, you read with horror a booming headline CRITIC FLAYS MAYOR'S NAIVE APPROACH. All you had said was that one of the mayor's comments sounded a bit naive. And your remark was only tossed off at the end of the interview.

The more sensational publications are likely to report you as responding angrily; lashing out; being sharply critical; issuing a blunt warning; attacking absurd proposals; expressing outrage; or otherwise declaring yourself pungently. So unless you are prepared for controversy, watch carefully every word you utter. Beware the unerasable throwaway line!

Don't agree to an interview by a sensational publication or a reporter known for her investigative journalism, unless you feel you can handle it. You would be advised anyway to ask for written questions and provide written answers.

Don't allow yourself to be interviewed by someone who clearly is a trainee or inexperienced reporter – let her cut her teeth on somebody else.

Unless you are very experienced, and are playing your own game of sowing seeds, don't give information off the record – it has a nasty habit of surfacing later, maybe from a far-off link in the journalistic chain.

Don't rush to answer. School yourself to let long pauses fall before you reply. Be alert – listen, listen, listen. What does each question mean? What may it be leading up to?

Don't be overawed. The reporter is not doing you a favour – you are doing her one. So stay in control. If she asks a question you are unsure about, don't make a stab – halt the interview and go to your files, or telephone a colleague. Get it right. If you cannot do so until later, refuse to answer on the spot and tell the reporter she will have to call back – or forego the information.

Of course, if you got a good indication of the subject matter she is interested in, you ought to have dug out a lot of useful information before she arrives. During that preparation time, make notes and mark passages in documents. Then, at the interview, stick to what you know, and don't guess.

Be careful about generalising from isolated instances – otherwise next day another reporter will demand that you provide your evidence, as a controversy begins to escalate. This is a common error – a trickle of instances is presented as if it were a flood.

Never rush to utter critical or snide remarks about named persons or organisations. Don't rely on the reporter to protect you against a lawsuit for defamation. Be aware that sometimes where you name no-one your remarks may be taken to refer to a particular person.

Can you ask to see the story before it is published? Yes – and almost certainly you will be refused. But you can make it a condition of being interviewed that you see the script or have it read to you over the phone; then the reporter has to decide whether to agree or not. If she does, you won't have the right to alter the script – but if she has got something factually wrong, you will have a good chance of persuading her to correct it before publication.

A word about speeches: when agreeing to speak at a public meeting, always ask whether the press will be present. This may cause you to tone down what you would otherwise say. Also, you can bring spare copies of your script (if you have one) and, most important, before the meeting you can invite them to see you afterward on any point they are unsure about. Where you are speaking only from trigger words on cards, you can give a reporter an interview afterwards, centred around those points.

Boiling It Down

For TV News

You can appear in a speaking role on TV in many ways: in a 30 second news item; in 3 to 5 minutes of pre-recorded (and probably heavily edited) comments as part of a current affairs programme; in a solo studio interview; in a group studio interview. Studio interviews sometimes also have an audience.

Being interviewed for TV news demands brevity and clarity.

You may be interviewed for only 60 seconds and edited down to 30. You must boil your case down to about half a dozen statements. Think in headlines – that is, short summary-style sentences. Try to make them colourful, evocative or entertaining. To be used, they must have impact.

Be ready to begin with your most arresting one-liner. Because of the need for brevity, the interviewer may enter an informal pact with you, telling you some or all of the questions he will ask and advising you which of your proposed answers would be too unwieldy.

If the interview is on location (say, in your home or office), a mike may be clipped to your clothing, voice levels taken, spotlights arranged, your phone taken off the hook, curtains drawn, items moved around on your desk. Just before the camera begins to roll, the interviewer may confide in you: 'My first question will be "Why do you think boxing should be banned?" Okay?' You nod, the camera rolls, the first question is asked, and you look the interviewer in the eye as you respond: 'You would have to be Attila the Hun to have enjoyed that gruesome bloodbath in last night's fight. Yet 800 Attilas roared their approval from the ringside. That's the first reason why boxing should be banned. It's as barbaric as cockfighting or bearbaiting.'

Having given your 'first reason' you have established a link with your next statement, and you continue at once: 'The second reason is that medical research shows all boxers suffer some degree of brain damage. I shudder to think what happened inside the skulls of those two fighters last night.'

Here you pause to let him come in with a question: 'But doesn't boxing teach self-defence and isn't that important when it is increasingly unsafe to walk the streets?'

'Rubbish,' you reply. 'Most of those 800 spectators last night will never box in their lives. Boxing teaches self-defence to very few: it teaches violence and cruelty to many.'

'But boxing administrators say the game has been cleaned up and made much safer than it used to be.'

You snort derisively. 'Was that tomato sauce covering those two gladiators last night? Did Kinghit Kelly go down twice merely to inspect the canvas – or was he half-unconscious?'

There the interviewer calls 'Cut'. He has several good pithy comments from you; but even so may not be able to use them all. That

145

emphasises the need for brevity. You may get only two or three sentences in an evening news bulletin: so you have to make them good.

Dealing With The
Longer TV Interview

Many TV interviews are entirely unthreatening: you are asked to describe your raft trip through wild rapids; how you train sheepdogs; what floodwaters did to your home; or the present state of the new-car market. All you have to do is be yourself, look directly at the interviewer, strike a conversational tone and tell your story in simple, everyday language. When preparing for such an interview, think of little anecdotes to relate – as in all forms of public speaking, audiences respond best if you tell a story or paint a picture. Generalisations bore viewers, but a brief anecdote captures their imagination.

But while many interviews are of this placid kind, others are probing, even abrasive, and you had better not treat them lightly. To find out how the interviewer thinks and prepares, I spoke to Brian Edwards, a formidable interviewer on television.

You are entitled to know, says he, the answers to these questions: who will your interviewer be; will the interview be live or pre-recorded; if pre-recorded, will it be edited; what length will it be; what will be the general question area; will anyone else be interviewed at the same time as you? All these things can affect either your decision to take part, or the nature of your preparation. 'Don't agree to appear if you feel the odds are stacked against you: too little time to prepare, too little information available, opposition too strong.'

Brian Edwards is master of the probing interview. He admits there is some subterfuge in the sparring that goes on prior to the event. Says he:

A skilful interviewer will be doing a lot to conceal the true nature of what's about to happen. To be perfectly frank about it, if I'm going to do an interview in which I think I've got some very strong ammunition, and it's going to be a very abrasive interview indeed, I will probably be extraordinarily pleasant and reassuring to that person outside the interview room. So there's a bit of deviousness that comes into it, and it would be foolish to deny it.

When do you discover the awful truth? Often, about question

number three. 'Generally speaking you're not going to throw in your big question at the beginning. You want them to relax a little bit; you probably want them to develop a sense of false security, so you will lead in gently.'

Then there's the innocent-sounding question that draws you into an awful mire. 'It's a chess game. The chess player doesn't think only of the move his opponent has just made. He thinks: "Where is that leading?" The interviewee must do the same. He must ask: "What's he building here?" That's often the case when you are asked what seem straight informational questions.'

So when the interviewer casually inquires whether you wrote a letter to Jeremiah Flogg on 28 March, you should be aware that a few questions later something in that letter is going to be made very awkward for you.

What does a person do who manages to evade the traps, even beat the interviewer? 'He will have a very good case and he will win by sheer reasonableness. He won't allow propositions to go past that aren't right. An interviewee who is holding his end up will be saying "Hold on a minute" quite a lot. He will be listening. It is a listening skill.'

So what do you do when after a few exploratory questions about your firm's dealing with old Mrs Wavering, the interviewer says accusingly: 'Why is your firm hounding this poor woman?'

Says Brian Edwards:

The more reasonable and low key you are, the more points you will win and also the more difficult you will make it for the interviewer to carry on being aggressive. So you say: 'I don't think we have been hounding this woman. I think that's quite the wrong word.' Or you can say: 'Would you like to give me an example of when we hounded this woman?' Or 'I don't think you have any evidence of our doing that. What evidence do you have?'

So far, fine. But what if the interviewer is probing your weak spot? What if your position is indefensible? Then make a gracious concession. Say frankly you have made a mistake and briefly what you intend doing to fix it. 'If you make a concession you defuse the interviewer in that area,' says Brian Edwards. 'You take the sting out of it.'

Also, you throw the interviewer onto his wits. He expected you to deny his charge, and the next five or six questions on his clipboard are intended to press you into an admission. When you con-

147

cede the point, not only do you win favour with the audience, but you derail the interviewer's train of thought. Since some interviews are really one-question interviews, your immediate capitulation on the central question prevents further damaging exploration of the same embarrassing point. Indeed, a quick admission can leave the interviewer no option but to delve into the remedial action you are taking, and the whole exercise may well be turned into good publicity rather than bad.

'Never try to defend the indefensible,' says Brian Edwards. And in particular beware the devastating effect of the closeup. Any squirming in your argument is likely to be reflected unmistakeably in your face. Says he:

It is an extraordinarily intimate medium and you are in a greater closeup on TV than you are in real life. You've got a camera which may on occasion come in from your hairline to just above your chin. The viewer can see everything and we are all to some extent reading body language – eye language and lip language. It doesn't really matter what you are saying, the viewer will know. This is one of the reasons why it is stupid to come along with a dishonest case, because the viewer will spot it.

Always, the camera is waiting. 'Many people do not realise that the camera may well be on them when they are not answering. The producer will know question three is the sticky question and the camera will be on you when it is asked. And your face will say, "Hell, how did he find that out?" Then you will give a nice confident smooth answer – but it's too late.'

Perhaps the single most important thing to appreciate is this: tomorrow or next week people will remember practically nothing of what you said – but they will remember how you came across. 'They remember the good story you told, the high-drama conflict, the spat (whichever side won), the general look on your face. They will forget most of your argument and will be left in the main with a general impression of you and your reasonableness – or lack of it.'

As a sideline Brian Edwards coaches people on how to present themselves on television:

When we train people, what we're trying to do is put them back the way they are in real life. What destroys people's performance on television is their fear. The main effect is they lose all their naturalness. They sit there in a very stiff way and they don't move and they don't speak the way they normally do.

So there it is. If you suspect you may be subjected to a probing TV interview, sit down with your colleagues and try to work out your weak spots and your answers to questions about them. Will you concede mistakes graciously, or do you have good explanations for apparent failings? Resolve firmly that you will not lose your cool in the interview; always you will try to give the impression of fairness and reasonableness, with no hint of evasion. You will not let untrue or unfairly slanted questions go without challenge – you will pull the interviewer back firmly. You will try to be natural, relaxed and conversational. You will choose simple language and everyday examples – not abstract or technical generalisations. You will try to be lively and humorous if you can.

Don't learn lines by rote. Get your argument clear, but don't try to memorise a series of statements, otherwise you will end up with what is known as 'scrambled brains', and will be unable to adapt to the ebb and flow of the questions.

Unless there's something important (a letter, for example) that you must quote, don't bring any notes with you – and bring no visual aids, because the camera cannot deal with them. Look at the interviewer, not at the camera, and try to think of it as a one-to-one conversation, shutting out everything else.

Don't wear black, white, garish colours or stripes. Restrained autumn tones are best. Lean forward, rather than back, because it gives an impression of interest and doesn't do nasty things with double chins. While waiting (and often there's a lot of waiting), be inquisitive and talkative because it gets your thoughts moving and prevents you dwelling upon your nervousness.

Is Radio Just TV
Without The Pictures?

For these purposes, radio can safely be described as 'TV without pictures'. But there are important differences. In radio interviews, people are likely to remember your words more than they do from TV. There is still not a high level of recall, though, and again you are likely to be remembered more for how you spoke than for what you said.

It's necessary to speak a little faster on radio than on TV, because there are no visual events to bridge gaps between sentences. Also, there is an even greater need to inject animation, enthusiasm and variety into your voice. For only through your voice do you project colour, energy and character. Think of it as chatting intimately with a friend. Be informal, sincere, and use simple words and concrete examples.

You must be concise – though never so brief as 'yes' or 'no'. Most often you will speak one to five sentences in answer to each question; then pause for the next.

For the rest, apply the advice laid down for television. Stand up for your rights as an interviewee. Don't be over-awed. Try to project yourself as believable, friendly and reasonable.

Summary

1. Say nothing until you know who will be asking you what, and for what purpose.

2. Don't hesitate to decline to be interviewed, and you need give no reason.

3. Take time to prepare if you can; decide what you can say and what you can not.

4. Don't let the interviewer take control.

5. Don't let loaded questions go past unchallenged.

6. Try to think the interviewer's thoughts – where may that innocent question lead you.

7. Don't defend the indefensible.

8. To concede a mistake may throw the interviewer, and allow you to convert bad publicity into good.

9. Keep your cool at all times; be polite before, during and after the interview.

10. On TV and radio it's not your words people remember, but a general impression of you and your reasonableness – or lack of it.

Part Three

WHAT YOU CAN LEARN FROM DEBATING

Chapter Eleven

BE FAMILIAR WITH THE
SKILLS OF DEBATE

When you argue over the back fence that your neighbour's favourite tree is blocking your view, you are debating. When you try
to persuade your reluctant boss to give you a raise, you are
debating. When you defend yourself against a careless driving
charge, you are debating. Whenever you find yourself in a formal
dispute, or even in a casual difference of opinion, you are debating.

And chances are, you will not do justice to your case. You may
fail to recognise the main issue; or try to prove more than you need
to; or ruin your case by introducing a weak argument that is
irrelevant to your purpose.

In this chapter we will discuss the skills of formal debate. It matters not at all that you may never debate competitively: if you
understand the skills involved you will be better equipped to put
your case on any issue; to marshal your evidence; to withstand challenges; to see the nub of an opposing point of view; to be alert to
dastardly tricks others may use against you.

What dastardly tricks? Here is a small selection of dishonest
methods of argument. They are common both in debates and in
everyday discourse.

Guilt by association. The speaker seeks to destroy his opponent's
arguments not by showing them to be wrong but by associating
them with unpopular or failed theories or with unpopular persons.
'What my opponent argues is just the sort of thing Adolf Hitler
would have proposed . . .'

Use of emotive terms. 'If you pander to the unions on this matter
. . .' is loaded by the use of the emotive term 'pander' (substitute
'agree with' and you will see how loaded the term is).

Exaggerating the effects. 'This proposal will wreck the economy,
throw tens of thousands out of work, cause untold riots and blood-
shed, and set our standard of living in ruins.'

Attacking the speaker instead of his argument. 'This is just the sort of proposal you would expect from such a fat-cat lawyer . . .'

Inventing an admission. When the Minister of Labour has announced a small increase in unemployment: 'The Minister has been forced to confess that his government's policies are hopelessly inadequate to contain runaway unemployment.' Of course, the Minister has confessed no such thing: the speaker puts his own words into the Minister's mouth.

All of these arguments, and dozens more, are encountered routinely in debates – and also in the everyday discussions of ordinary people.

So I urge you to become familiar with debating skills. They are indispensable to all good communicators.

What Is Debating?

A formal debate is an argument over an issue, played out within a set of rules. There are two teams. The Affirmative support the subject of the debate; the Negative oppose it. Any number of people may take part (I once participated in a twelve-a-side event), but normally there are either two or three in each team. Sometimes all the debaters will speak only once; sometimes all will speak twice; but mostly all will speak once with team leaders summarising at the end.

The principles of debating are the same, whatever the format. In this chapter I will use as my example two teams of three people. Each of the six debaters speaks for ten minutes, and then the two leaders summarise for six minutes each.

In any debate, skills of presentation are as important as the material used. A persuasive, commanding, confident debater who has moderately good material will often defeat a halting, colourless, timid opponent who has much better material. But since presentation (use of voice, gesture, stance, eye contact, and so on) has been examined in Chapter 6, we will ignore it here. In this chapter we will discuss the debating *case* and how it is structured. In particular, we will deal with the five elements that can be memorised as DEARS: Definition, Evidence, Argument, Rebuttal and Summary. We will take each of these elements one by one.

D – FOR DEFINITION

In a debate, everything revolves around the motion. The motion can also be known as the proposition, the proposal, the moot, or simply the subject. Motions are never a single word (*Strikes*) but always a formally worded proposition (*That the Right to Strike Should be Abolished*).

The wording of the motion sets out the battleground for the debate. This cannot be stressed too strongly. When defining the motion you must understand clearly what each significant word means, and you will need to use a good dictionary with care.

From time to time the motion is loosely worded – such as, *That the Answer Lies in the Soil*. This motion is capable of ten or fifteen interpretations.

– *That the nation should farm its way out of its economic difficulties.*
– *That people should abandon the cities and look for a better life back on the land.*
– *That people should all work harder – that is, soil their hands for the good of the nation.*
– *That ideas of a dead person whose bones lie in the soil (e.g. Lincoln, Marx, Aristotle) are needed to solve present-day problems.*
– *That we should all dig underground shelters as the only answer to the threat of nuclear warfare.*
And so on.

Such vague motions place a heavy burden on the Negative. Since it is impossible to predict which way the Affirmative will go, the Negative must prepare or part-prepare at least half a dozen cases and will not know the central issue of the debate until the Affirmative leader is part-way through his opening speech.

Vague motions invite the Affirmative to twist the meaning in an attempt to wrong-foot the Negative. This leads to a tedious wrangle over definition throughout the contest – to the disgust of audience and adjudicator who want to hear the *issue* disputed, not the meaning of the motion.

I strongly advise you not to twist the meaning of the motion. This alienates your listeners, often comes unstuck, and hardly identifies you as the fearless, take-them-as-you-come debater you ought to be. It is best to accept the most obvious meaning of the subject, and meet your opponents head-on.

How To Identify The Two
Main Types Of Motion

Some textbooks will tell you the 'burden of proof' lies with the

Affirmative, since it is they who are proposing the motion. *Not* true. The burden of proof is always shared. The Negative must at least prove their challenge to the Affirmative case, and in some instances they will put forward an alternative case of their own which they must also prove. As we shall see, proof (and disproof) is presented by way of evidence and argument – and any Negative team that fails to produce its own evidence and argument will almost certainly lose.

To decide what has to be proved, especially by the Affirmative, you need to analyse the motion with great care. Broadly, there are two main types of motion:

1. The motion that makes a *judgement* about a situation and seeks the audience's agreement with that judgement: *That People Get the Politicians They Deserve,* or *That the Welfare State has Sapped Our Initiative,* or *That the Pleasures of the Flesh are Over-Rated.*

2. The motion that proposes a *change* to a situation and seeks the audience's agreement to that change: *That Mercy Killing Should Be Legalised,* or *That All Workers Should Work a Thirty-Hour Week,* or *That Everyone Should Be Taught Karate.*

Let's discuss these two types of motion in some detail.

The Motion that Makes a Judgement. This type of motion may involve a factual judgement (*That Western Civilisation is on the Brink of Collapse*), or a moral judgement (*That Political Injustice Justifies a Violent Response*) or a combination of the two (*That the Atom Bomb Should Never Have Been Used on Hiroshima*).

Where the motion makes a judgement about a situation, the Affirmative has two things to prove:

(a) It must say what are the standards for making such a judgement and convince the audience that the chosen standards are indeed the correct ones.

(b) It must prove that those standards are met, or are met sufficiently, in the case in question. That is, it must persuade the audience to accept the judgement that is made in the motion.

For example, take the subject: *That the Government has Failed.* The Affirmative may choose these standards against which to measure success or failure: the economy, external trade, employment, industrial relations, foreign policy, social welfare and business confidence. Having established the standards it will use, the Affirmative goes on to provide evidence of failure in respect of each

156

standard. If the government is clearly doing well in one aspect (say, in fighting inflation), the Affirmative will seek to play down this success: 'Of course the Government has reduced inflation – but look at the cost. Its anti-inflationary policies have thrown multitudes out of work, collapsed entire industries and driven tens of thousands of citizens below the poverty line. Meanwhile our external trade has gone to the dogs, our foreign policy is in disarray, and industrial relations is a disaster area . . .'

To combat this line, the Negative will probably choose different standards (say, education and housing), where the government's performance is better. Not for a moment will they concede that the government's good performance in lowering inflation is irrelevant. They will argue that the tide is turning – the government is putting policies in place, beginning with the successful attack on inflation, that will mean a better life for all in future.

The Negative, therefore, may attack the choice of standards, or argue that the standards are not met sufficiently in the present case – or perhaps they may argue both lines. They may also set up an alternative case, arguing that the opposition party would do a better job than the government. However, that tactic would be unwise: as a general rule, neither team should attempt to prove more than it has to, because this gives its opponents a bigger target to shoot at. Usually the Negative should only consider proffering a case of its own when the Affirmative's case is difficult to challenge.

The Motion that Proposes Change. The other main type of motion proposes a *change* in a situation. This requires the Affirmative to prove three things:

(a) That something is so seriously wrong with the situation that a change is essential.

(b) That the change proposed by the Affirmative will fix the problems in the situation, and that any disadvantages introduced by the change will be outweighed by the good effects.

(c) That no other method of altering the situation would be preferable to the one proposed.

Let's take this subject: *That Women Should Run the Country.* The Affirmative must prove (a) that men are doing the job badly, (b) that women would do it better and (c) that there is no more preferable way of altering the situation. Almost certainly the Negative will attack at point (c), arguing that the running of the country should be shared equally by men and by women. They will agree men are doing a bad job, and will dispute that women, alone, could do a good job. This is the sensible Negative case, but a different response could easily enough be mounted, arguing that men may not be doing an ideal job, but women would do far worse.

When faced with a motion that proposes a change in a situation, the Negative may:

(a) Argue that the situation is not bad.

(b) Accept that the situation is bad, but argue that the proposed solution will not improve it, or will introduce disadvantages that outweigh the advantages.

(c) Accept that the situation is bad, but argue that another solution (not proposed by the Affirmative) is better than the one they do propose.

Identifying the Type
Of Motion

What you have to prove depends largely on whether the motion makes a *judgement* or proposes a *change*. It is especially important to know whether change is proposed. For one thing, you need to consider who in the community is suggesting change – if nobody is (or nobody of any consequence) you can expect to be harried unmercifully by the Negative demanding to know where is the informed body of opinion that advocates change.

Often, the word 'ought' or 'should' in the motion indicates change. So too do the words 'is necessary', 'is needed' and 'is desirable'. But not always. Despite use of the word 'should', the motion *That Our Grandchildren Should Be Pitied* simply makes a *judgement* about the future of mankind.

Sometimes the distinction is not clear. *That Parliament is a Farce* could be taken to mean it is unavoidably so and cannot be improved (judgement only); or that it should be reformed (advocating change). Similarly, *That We Pamper the Elderly* could mean that we spoil them and they deserve to be spoiled (judgement only); or that we spoil them unduly and they should be given less (which advocates a change). Adding 'too much' to this motion (*That We Pamper the Elderly Too Much*) introduces a presumption that change is advocated. Often, the presence of the word 'too' indicates change – *That There Are Too Many Laws* implies the number should be reduced.

We have now dealt with Definition, the first of the five principles that spell DEARS. Next, we shall look at Evidence.

E – FOR EVIDENCE

Once you have established a definition of the motion, you will need to work out your case – that is, your line of argument. Whether Affirmative or Negative, you must have a case, and it is essential to find good evidence to support that case.

Evidence is facts or opinions, and sometimes even physical objects (e.g. photos).

Argument takes the evidence and shows how it proves the case.

The business of debate is *proof* and *disproof* – both of which require these two elements: evidence and argument.

Let's look first at what happens in the absence of evidence. Then you have empty assertion, which often is introduced thus:

– *Everyone knows . . .*
– *Scientists have proved . . .*
– *It is a fact . . .*
– *No-one can deny . . .*

Phrases such as these are dishonest attempts to give some status or backing to the assertion that follows. If an assertion sounds precise, it seems to be more than an assertion: 'The level of unemployment among school leavers is now 20 per cent.' But if this bald statement is unsupported, it is indeed merely assertion.

It is quite another matter if the debater says: 'The latest employment statistics as given at page 23 of last month's *Labour and Employment Gazette* show that just under 20 per cent of children who left school in December were still unemployed four months later.' With this statement he or she has presented a solid piece of evidence (which is capable of being either verified or challenged by going to the quoted source). This evidence can then be used as persuasive support for his case (say, *That Reducing Inflation Produces Unacceptable Levels of Unemployment*).

Sadly, too many debates – and everyday arguments – are marred by the toss and counter-toss of assertion. Loose statements abound in our speech. No wonder prejudice and bias are so rife: far too many people leap to conclusions without bothering to gather evidence (pro and con) first.

Evidence as used in a court of law has specialised meaning, and I do not concern myself with that. Here, I want to discuss the kinds of evidence used in debate: (1) examples or instances; (2) personal anecdotes: (3) statistics; (4) expert opinion; (5) ordinary opinion; (6) illustrations; (7) common knowledge.

1. *Examples.* If you are trying to prove *That Adversity Strengthens Resolve,* you may give the example of a famous author who starved in a garret for years before writing her great novel. Isolated instances such as this are not telling (except as illustration of a trend that you will prove by stronger evidence), so usually you need to gather a number of such examples before they become useful.

2. *Statistics.* If sound, up-to-date and relevant, statistics can be very persuasive. If you can quote a statistical survey that shows more than 80 per cent of paraplegics display increased determination to do well at sport after suffering their disabilities, that is splendid evidence for your case.

3. *Personal anecdote.* Telling how your old Mum survived widowhood, bushfires, a broken neck, penury and loss of her home in a flood, yet still brought up eight children to be saintly geniuses is of limited value. But if you have a special knowledge, your personal anecdote may be useful evidence: if you are industrial relations manager of your firm, giving your experiences in dealing with strikes may be helpful in a debate on that subject.

4. *Expert opinion.* This can be very persuasive, especially where your expert is well known, and you build him up well: 'I want now to quote from one of the world's foremost authorities on human sexuality, Professor Joseph Ogle. In his standard reference work, *The Oomph Factor,* he says at page 327: . . .' Preferably, you should quote several authorities all saying the same thing. Where a conference of experts has made a joint statement, this can be powerful evidence.

5. *Ordinary opinion.* Especially where multiplied, as in a public opinion poll, this too can be telling: 'In this month's Abacus Poll, nearly half those surveyed said inflation was the nation's number one problem.'

6. *Illustrations.* Telling a story ('painting a picture') can be very forceful in driving home a line of argument. Say, the description of a particularly brutal murder as part of a debate about violence in the

community. Such illustrations can heighten the impact of statistics and expert opinion on the subject.

7. *Common knowledge*. Some facts are so well known that they do not need verification, though it may be wise in some instances to say: 'As we have all read in the newspapers recently . . .'

This last form of evidence is of great importance. You cannot laboriously verify every statement you make, and no-one would be grateful if you tried. You must assume a certain amount of knowledge on the part of your audience. Thus you will verify with evidence only the key points you wish to make – plus some of your lesser arguments where common knowledge cannot be relied upon for support.

It need hardly be said that the quality of your evidence is more important than its mass. As we will see later, weak evidence invites slaughter by your opponents.

In most debates you will find yourself using a combination of evidence: statistics, expert opinion, common knowledge, examples, illustrations – all united to prove your case.

A – FOR ARGUMENT

We have dealt with the first two essentials of debate, as noted by the acronym DEARS. Now we come to Argument.

In my observation, the single most common fault among debaters is irrelevance. Many talented debaters are limited by poor understanding of the difference between evidence and argument. With much confidence and gusto they toss out sheaves of evidence, yet fail to show how those facts prove the motion (in the case of the Affirmative) or disprove it (in the case of the Negative).

Argument takes evidence (facts and opinions) and uses it to compel belief in your case. Argument is the 'reason why' your case should be believed. Indeed, argument is reasoning: you provide proof, by way of logic and evidence, for acceptance of your case.

Expressed in layperson's language, the four main types of argument used in debate are:

1. *Drawing inferences from signs or indicators*. 'Canadian troops are massing on the border of the United States, so we can conclude that invasion is imminent.' This argument rests on the widely held assumption that massing of troops is a sign of threat. (Probably not

so in this instance: the massed troops may be engaged in harmless manoeuvres.)

2. *Generalising from particular examples.* 'Church groups in Shanty-town report a dramatic increase in the numbers of unemployed people seeking food parcels – clear proof that dole payments are too low.' This argument rests on the assumption that examples of people queueing for food demonstrate financial hardship. (Possibly not so in this instance: the increase in requested food parcels may simply reflect recent publicity about the availability of the parcels.)

3. *Pointing to cause and effect.* 'Cutting back on inflation reduces the amount of money for purchase of consumer goods, and falling sales throw people out of work. So reducing inflation is undesirable because it will mean unacceptable levels of unemployment.' This argument rests on the assumption that a cause-and-effect relationship exists between levels of inflation and levels of unemployment. (Possibly not so in this instance: other facts such as migration increases may provide extra demand to keep employment figures stable.)

4. *Drawing an analogy.* 'The following were the key characteristics of the ancient Roman Empire before the collapse . . . the same characteristics are found in Western civilisation today . . . so there can be no doubt that our civilisation is on the point of collapse.' This argument rests on the assumption that parallel characteristics produce parallel results. (Very dubious in this instance: an analogy can hardly be sustained in the light of vast changes in world population, natural resources, scientific discovery, general knowledge, communications and political institutions, since Roman times.)

Debates commonly involve a mixture of types of argument. In particular, generalisations drawn from particular examples will be combined with different forms of causal argument. It is not surprising that in the hurly-burly of the developing dispute, thin and tangled arguments may be presented – as well as the deliberately crafty ones. As a result, it takes years for most people to become skilled at the art of logical argument.

Debaters often suffer not so much from bad argument as no argument. A speaker may pitch all manner of stirring facts at his audience, yet neglect to say what those facts prove or disprove. He assumes the audience will make the necessary connections between his facts and the motion. Of course all debates (and everyday discussions) are full of assumptions. Many of these assumptions are unavoidable (otherwise conversation would be bogged down by the need to prove every statement). But others loom too large and too dubious to be taken for granted. The debater must then use argument to knit the evidence into his case.

To do this, you need to cultivate the habit of using expressions such as these:
- *What this shows is* . . .
- *This fact proves* . . .
- *You can see from this statement that* . . .
- *This evidence demonstrates* . . .
- *So we must conclude that* . . .

These and similar phrases are the linkages that bridge evidence and argument, turning a jumble of facts into a reasoned case. *Because, therefore, thus* are other linkages.

In the reasoning process you show relationships between ideas and draw conclusions from established facts. Whether those conclusions are drawn validly from the facts is determined by logic.

This is not the place to deal with formal logic. But every thinking person should, however, have some knowledge of the principles of reasoning and of dishonest methods of argument.

Rarely in any dispute will you be treated to rigorous logic. There will be *some* evidence and *some* argument, intermingled with emotive statements, appeals to the beliefs of the listener, and many other persuasive devices. To take an extreme example: two people who enjoy titillating gossip meet to discuss 'the latest news about Alfred and Elena'. The teller needs little evidence or argument to persuade the listener: a conspiratorial manner and a flood of unsupported assertions will be quite sufficient to compel belief.

So too it is with any audience. If a speaker knows the attitudes, prejudices or cherished ideals of his hearers, he can, if he chooses, play to those factors to greater effect than merely piling up rigorous proof.

Indeed, whether an audience believes a speaker may depend comparatively little on proof. As discussed in Chapter 6, skills of persuasion can be much more effective than logic: an air of sincerity, an impression of fairness and balance, pleasing use of humour, compelling imagery, identification with the audience, a confident and likeable manner.

All this has been part of public utterances for thousands of years, and will continue to be. Yet debaters (and others) need to know the basics of argument, not only for the better presentation of their own case, but also because such understanding makes for better rebuttal.

R – FOR REBUTTAL

If there is one thing that distinguishes debating from all other forms of speaking, it is rebuttal. Without rebuttal there is only the pretence of debate: the audience is listening to a collection of prepared speeches, nothing more.

Debate implies collision between two points of view; the shredding of your opponents' case and the shoring up of your own. This interaction between teams, this clawing and jabbing and tearing at the opposing evidence and argument, is done by way of rebuttal.

Debates are seldom won because one team puts up a better *con*structive case than the other. More often, victory goes to the team that puts up the better *de*structive case, using superior rebuttal to destroy, or severely damage, the case put up by their opponents.

To rebut effectively you must do three things:

1. You must quote, correctly, those words of your opponents that you dispute. ('The second speaker of the Affirmative told us that social workers had found five local families living in disused sewer pipes.')

2. Then you must say precisely where he was wrong. ('What he did not say was that those families are members of a strict religious cult who renounce material possessions; and who had refused homes that were offered to them.')

3. Finally, you must say what is the significance of his error. ('So this so-called major piece of evidence fails completely to support the Affirmative's argument that there is a severe housing shortage.')

This third requirement is often overlooked. It is the same error that is so frequently made in the *con*structive material of a debating speech. The debater presents some evidence (in this case rebuttal evidence) but fails to add argument to show the significance of his evidence for the proving or disproving of the motion. You must tie everything that is said back to the issue in dispute.

Why do so many debaters rebut badly? Partly because they do not understand the function of rebuttal. But also because they have not thought enough about the case their opponents are likely to present. As a general rule, you should spend about half your preparation working out what your opponents might say, and your counter to it.

Of course, you won't be lucky enough to predict all the arguments and evidence your opponents will use. So you will need to concentrate carefully during the debate, in order to pick out major points as they occur, then rapidly prepare your rebuttal before it is your turn to speak. My debating team knows it will learn the main thrust of its opponents' case during the first half of their leader's opening speech. So we listen and wait, and if we have predicted well, observers will see our faces light up as we whisper to each other: 'They are going for case No. 2.' Then all of our thinking will be concentrated upon our rebuttal of Case No. 2. But that doesn't stop us *listening* as our opponents develop their line. This is a major trap: many debaters do not 'hear' enough of what the opposition is saying because they are too engrossed in their own case.

I cannot stress this too strongly: your team must grasp the main line of its opponents' case as quickly as it can. Then you must stay with their developing argument. It is easy to slide into silent rehearsal of your own case, missing vital evidence and argument your opposition is piling up.

The Two Main
Methods Of Rebuttal

The two main methods of rebuttal are:

1. Destructive rebuttal. This destroys the truth, validity or significance of your opponent's evidence or argument. You will show that his statistics are inaccurate; that the 'authority' he quotes is suspect; that his evidence doesn't prove what he claims it proves; and so on.

2. Parallel (or constructive) rebuttal. This doesn't destroy your opponent's evidence or argument (which may be irrefutable) but puts up opposing evidence to show the opposite. Thus, on the motion *That This is God's Own Country,* you know the Affirmative will point to beautiful lakes, rivers, forests and the like. You know they will cite examples that will be irrefutable. So you rebut by saying:

The Leader of the Affirmative told us that Lake Exquisite is a joy to behold and that Mount Awesome National Park is a heaven on earth. But what he avoided telling you is that Lake Emerald has become a sewer and that Green Belt National Park is soon to be opened up to logging. This may once have been God's Own Country but the gradual destruction of its physical beauty has reached the point where that can no longer be said . . .

Parallel rebuttal allows you to challenge the seemingly irrefutable, so it is of utmost importance. It is often known as 'weaving your own material into rebuttal of the other team's case'. Yet too many debaters use their own material only for *co*nstructive purposes, and may end up failing to rebut at all. It is essential not only to use your rebuttal well, but also to use both destructive and parallel rebuttal.

Three Main Types
Of Rebuttal

There are three main types of rebuttal:

1. *Rebuttal of the arguments of your opponents* (especially the main thrust of their case). Since such rebuttal can be very damaging, it is essential to tease it out, repeat it, ram it down their throats. Be scathing, scornful, dismissive – you have your knife at the heart of their case and must not fail to plunge it in. Whatever else you do, never skip lightly over a devastating piece of rebuttal. Make sure also that you show its significance.

You can attack:

(a) Weak, incomplete or inaccurate definition of the motion. Usually this is very effective. Your opponents are dodging the issue, you will say, by evading or distorting part of the definition.

(b) Inconsistency by a speaker who says one thing in part of his speech, then makes a contradicting statement in another. If this inconsistency is serious, your rebuttal can be devastating as you show he doesn't know what line to take.

(c) Inconsistency between speakers. Often in the hurly-burly of debate one of your opponents will inadvertently contradict something said by a team-mate. Again if the issue is major, you can make much mischief by showing they are quarrelling with each other and that their case is in disarray.

(d) Shifting ground. Where your opponents subtly change the emphasis of their case, you can often score by showing they started out arguing one line and now are presenting another.

(e) Loose assumptions. If you look again at the four types of argument given at page 161 you will see that each of them involves a suspect assumption. Experienced debaters look for dubious assumptions to challenge.

(f) Bad logic. Often a debater's argument does not prove what he or she claims it proves, and it is devastating to reveal this.

(g) Poor analysis. If your opponents have not· analysed the motion well (as one of *judgement* or *change*), you will have a merry time rebutting their failure of analysis.

2. *Rebuttal of evidence.* Spend time on rebutting *major* evidence, if your refutation is telling. Destruction of a significant piece of evidence will jolt your opposition's case; it will force them to spend time on counter-rebuttal; and they will end up highly defensive and shaken.

Rebuttal of *minor evidence* is often not worth the time, effort, and distraction from main issues. But if you can be really scathing, and can do it quickly, by all means crack the whip across their backs. But don't get bogged down in minor-point rebuttal. Equally, ignore red herrings dragged across your path by the opposition. Save your rebuttal time for the stuff that most damages the central thrust of their case.

Whether the evidence is major or minor, there are many possibilities of attack:

You may be able to show your opponents' evidence is: out of date; superseded by newer information; irrelevant; self-contradictory; insufficient; relies on hearsay; is largely assertion; comes from an unreliable source; is taken misleadingly out of context; is untypical; doesn't prove what it is claimed to prove.

Expert opinion may be attacked by showing: that the claimed expert is not an expert; that he is expert on some subjects but not the one on which he is quoted; that he is biased; that he has made other statements in contradiction to the one quoted; that he has been misquoted; that he has been misreported by the media; that his views have been rubbished by other experts.

Statistics and public opinion polls can be attacked by showing that the sample on which they are based is too small; that the sample is biased; that the questions asked were ambiguous; that the questions were phrased to nudge respondents towards the desired answer; that a statistical series would show a different trend if begun in a different year from the one chosen.

3. *Counter-rebuttal*. This is your response to rebuttal that your opponents have directed at your own team's evidence or argument. It is essential, if you can, to re-establish your team's main line of argument, if it has been shaken. And essential, too, to defend a major piece of evidence that has been damaged. The art of counter-rebuttal is to mount a further attack when re-establishing your point that has been damaged by the opposition.

Not only does counter-rebuttal patch up holes that have been knocked in your case; it also demonstrates teamwork, for it usually involves support for a preceding teammate.

As in rebuttal so in counter-rebuttal – don't waste powder and shot (and precious time) countering minor damage inflicted by the other team. Most inexperienced debaters feel they must respond to every assault made upon them and end up flailing about in wild retaliation with the result they are left with insufficient time to build their own case. You must learn to take punches. Accept that the other team will score points. Your job is to score more than they do. So be selective about counter-rebuttal: shore up only key arguments and key evidence that have been damaged; ignore all else.

And, of course, if a key point of your team has been so demolished that it can hardly be restored, don't waste time trying to counter-rebut, for the weakness of your response will simply draw further attention to the strength of your opponents' attack.

Counter-rebuttal can be done, broadly, in two ways:

First by re-establishing the damaged point. This is done by showing your opponents were devious, or mistaken, or selective, in their attack.

Second by piling on more evidence of a similar kind to re-establish the original evidence that your opponents have attacked.

S – FOR SUMMARY

At the end of the main speeches the team leaders speak again, but this time the Negative leader precedes the Affirmative. Thus is balance restored: the Affirmative leader is given the 'final say' in recompense for having no attacking opportunities in his opening speech.

In your summary, you lay out the key points of your opponents' case and show how your own team demonstrated that case to be wrong. Then you lay out the key points of your own team's case, and show how your opponents failed to do significant damage.

Normally, you will spend half your time on what is wrong with the other team's case and half on what is right with yours, ending with a short peroration that re-presents your case dramatically.

The rules of debate normally specify that no new material may be presented in a summary, though a skilful leader can often weave in new material without appearing to do so. For example, if his second speaker has used some evidence but failed to draw a clear conclusion from that evidence, his leader may restate the evidence and adroitly draw the desired conclusion from it. Or if his third speaker used only one piece of a two-part segment of material, the leader may be able to slip the missing piece in while summarising that part of his team's case.

Often summaries are abysmally scrappy events in which the speaker wastes time on minor issues, takes up red herrings laid for him by the opposition, responds to empty challenges, and generally fails to demonstrate mastery of what has taken place.

Make sure you answer the main thrust of your opponents' case (e.g. 'The Affirmative's case can be reduced to these three main propositions . . .'). And then demonstrate clearly where the essence of their argument went wrong. You may home in on their weak or incomplete definition; demonstrate inconsistencies between the arguments of their team members; show that their case was modified and shifted ground as the debate progressed; that crucial pieces of evidence were destroyed by your team; that key points were supported by nothing more than assertion; that important evidence they put forward actually proves *your* team's case.

When summarising your own case, again ignore points of detail. And disregard weak attacks upon you, and attacks on minor evidence you put forward. Concentrate on the main thrust of your case, how solid was the major evidence supporting it, and how weak the attack upon it. Counter-rebut if you can any significant attack by your opponents on your main line of argument or on a major piece of your evidence.

Two final pieces of advice: first, make sure you know your own team's case thoroughly and prepare your summary of it in advance; this allows you to concentrate on summarising the other team's case as it develops. Second, watch your use of time. With depressing frequency, a leader spends too much time summarising his opponents' weaknesses (real or supposed) and then has to scamper hastily through a summary of his own team's strengths (real or supposed).

Summary

Some common faults of debate are:

1. Poor understanding of the five essentials of debate: Definition, Evidence, Argument, Rebuttal and Summary (DEARS).

2. Failure to analyse the motion thoroughly to discover what the Affirmative is required to prove and the Negative to disprove.

3. Spending insufficient time anticipating your opponents' case and your counter to it.

4. A poor understanding of the difference between evidence and argument.

5. Irrelevance – failure to show how your evidence proves or disproves the motion.

6. Reliance on assertion.

7. Failure to adapt to the developing arguments of your opponents.

8. Inadequate or ineffective rebuttal.

9. Poor presentation.

Chapter Twelve

HOW TO DEVELOP
ADVANCED METHODS OF ARGUMENT

At about the same time as the Watergate scandal was approaching its climax, my debating team reached the final of a major competition. The motion we were presented with was: *That Richard Nixon Deserves Our Sympathy*. To our dismay, we were required to support this proposition. Even at the time the motion was decided upon, it seemed impossible to affirm. But one month later, when the day of the debate had arrived, there had been so many further revelations of unsavoury behaviour that we wondered whether we ought simply to concede and avoid ignominious defeat!

Yet we won. How that victory was achieved is instructive. There are at least six major meanings of the word sympathy. We chose compassion. The motion, we said, meant that people should feel sorry for Richard Nixon. But first we had to make clear we were not defending his innocence. The very first words we used when opening the debate were:

President Richard Nixon has been accused of illegal and immoral activities and day by day the demand swells that he be thrown out of office. Very probably the allegations are true. Very probably Richard Nixon has been involved in a cover-up of illegal activities. Very probably he has lied to the American people. Very probably he has been guilty of crimes for which he could be convicted at law.

By now the Negative were looking at each other in consternation, whispering furiously, obviously unable to understand what we were up to. Our case continued:

But that is not the issue in this debate. It is possible to feel compassion for someone who has behaved badly. It is possible for a man guilty of despicable crimes still to be deserving of sympathy.

In brief, our case is: Richard Nixon is deserving of sympathy because he has been subjected to trial by media as no other person in history. He risks

171

having wrenched from his grasp the possession he cherishes above all others: the presidency of the United States. No man has been so remorselessly hounded, badgered and tormented before the eyes of so many millions of people. Day by day the most powerful figure on earth has been pursued by a ravening pack of bloodthirsty wolves, numbering not hundreds, but millions, even tens of millions. He is a lion at bay. Whatever crimes he may have committed there is tragedy in the humiliation of this towering figure. As bit by bit his flesh is rent by his tormentors, we can see that this is not justice; it is slow, agonising death. This is not application of the rule of law; it is retribution by lynch mob; it is trial by media on a global scale. Because of that, because he has been subjected to lynch law to a monstrous degree, because he is in the process of being dragged from the greatest heights to the lowest depths, because he is already a figure of tragedy worthy of a Greek play — we say he deserves our (and your) sympathy.

This line staggered the Negative. They were thrown into such disarray they never recovered. Throughout their preparation they had assumed we would argue Nixon deserved sympathy because he was innocent: that whatever Nixon's men had done, it was without his knowledge or connivance.

Faced with so perilous a motion, our team knew surprise was our only ally. Had the Negative gathered their wits in time they would have found our theme seriously suspect. It was all very well for us to inveigh against trial by media; but in fact the Watergate scandal would never have been revealed had it not been for the staunch tenacity of the news media generally, and of those remarkable *Washington Post* reporters, Woodward and Bernstein, in particular.

So there it was. We on the Affirmative, who harboured in our breasts not one jot of sympathy for Nixon, acted as advocates for tens of millions of Americans who believed unswervingly (many of them to this day) that he was treated unjustly over Watergate.

The lesson here is that, even when faced with seemingly impossible odds, you may save the day for the point of view you represent, by tactics and good generalship.

An even more important lesson was set before the Negative. Though surely presented with the 'right' point of view to represent, they let an overwhelming case be stolen away because they did not anticipate, neglected to put themselves in the shoes of their opponents, and failed to adopt a flexible strategy.

Here now are some advanced tactics you can use.

Turning Their Evidence
To Your Advantage

It is always devastating to demonstrate that a much-touted piece of evidence fails to prove what your opponents have claimed for it. Let's suppose the motion is *That Petrol Rationing Should Be Introduced For All Motorists.* As their main challenge to this proposition, the Negative argue that it is unnecessary to burden all motorists with rationing – instead, the government should simply curb the profligate users. They make much fuss of a forthcoming car racing meeting: 'Just consider how much petrol will be squandered by all those racing cars whizzing around the track for hours. It is madness to starve essential users of petrol while permitting such waste.'

It seems a persuasive argument. But the Affirmative are unfazed. Using the simplest arithmetic they total the petrol that will be used by the racing cars *and* by the spectators who drive to the car-racing meeting. Then with a flourish they ask the audience to consider a *horse-racing* meeting that will be held on the same day. With evident satisfaction they calculate the amount of petrol that will be used in transporting both horses and spectators to the event. Since there will be many more spectators at the horse races, the total petrol used in staging that event will be far greater than the total petrol used at the car races. With heavy sarcasm they ask whether the horse-racing event should be abandoned too, plus the movies, the ballet, the roller-skating and every other event which spectators attend by car.

This rebuttal accepts the Affirmative's evidence, but ruins its argument by showing the evidence does not help to prove the motion.

Sometimes evidence used by your opponents can be turned to your own team's advantage by demonstrating that it supports your own case. On the motion *That Farmers Have Got It Easy,* the Affirmative may rail against massive farm subsidies paid by the taxpayer. No other sector is so cocooned against economic adversity, they say, and this is clear proof that farmers have got things easy. Not so, counters the Negative: even after large subsidies are added in, average incomes of farmers are still modest and are less than those of manufacturers, importers and professional groups. Turning the evidence to their own advantage, the Negative declare: 'The fact that large subsidies have to be paid is clear proof that farmers do *not* have things easy. These subsidies show how sick farming is; it is only subsidies that keep farmers on the land; in this way an un-economic sector is kept going in order to maintain food supply and prevent widespread rural unemployment.'

Putting Pressure On
Your Opponents

Let's suppose you are affirming *That Literary Censorship Should Be Abolished*. The leader of the Negative strides to the platform carrying a stool and several sheets of typescript. With a flourish, he deposits the stool before him and places the pages of typescript face down upon the stool, and begins:

Ladies and gentlemen, the Affirmative leader has told you there is no need for mature adults to be told what they may or may not read. He says there should be no censorship whatever of reading material sold to adults. Well we of the Negative have a challenge for him. We have taken extracts from four books currently on sale. There they are, on the stool before me. We challenge the next Affirmative speaker to pick up any of those extracts and read it to you in a loud, clear voice. If they are right – that there is no need for censorship – then there is no reason why they shouldn't read to you, as a group of mature adults, whatever is written on any of those pages.

You are the next Affirmative speaker. What should you do? Without doubt, if you pick up one of the pages you will find it contains an appallingly obscene and/or sadistic account. Very probably you will gag upon the words when halfway through and discard the script in confused dismay. That of course would be disastrous. But to ignore the challenge would be almost as fatal to your case. What is the way out?

Simply this: walk calmly out from behind the table. Say plainly:

Well, that's a tired old trick the Negative have dredged up in their desperation. They know perfectly well our case is that adults should have the right to read pornographic material – not that it should be forced upon them. So if any of you wishes to read those extracts at the end of the debate, feel free to do so. But since some of you will not wish to be exposed to such material, I am not going to read it out. Actually, I am grateful to the Negative for helping me to illustrate the essence of our case – that those in the community (or in this audience) who wish to read pornographic material should be able to do so, without disturbing the right of others to shun such material.

Usually, a challenge has to be met, for to let it go unanswered is damaging. But try to meet it on your terms, not on those of the challenger.

Should you issue challenges of your own? Yes, by all means. But be aware that if your challenge is answered well, you will be weakened, for in issuing it you showed that you thought it an important point. I always think it better not to use the term 'challenge'. Instead, use such expressions as: 'The Affirmative must tell us . . .' Then, if they don't, your leader can say in his summary: 'We challenged the Affirmative to tell us . . .' and he can make much of their failure to respond.

One common challenge is to demand that a speaker 'table his authority', which means that the book or newspaper clipping he is quoting from should be placed on the chairman's table as proof that the quotation is accurate (or even that it exists!) It is always bad tactics to table your authority. Immediately the leader of the other team will grab the material from the chairman's table and hand it to his second speaker with the terse instruction: 'Find something'. And sure enough, on most occasions he will discover another quote from the same material that can be used against his opponents! So don't give the other side any ammunition. The best response, when challenged to table your authority is: 'Do your own research! We've done ours and we are not going to hand it to you.'

Challenges are frequently used to put pressure on the opponent who follows you: 'The next speaker must answer the following points . . .' Putting pressure on your opponents is an important tactic in any debate. Often the third Negative will challenge the Affirmative leader to reply to a particular point in his summary – the purpose being to disrupt that summary. (This cannot be done to the Negative leader because any challenge by the third Affirmative will be answered by the third Negative.)

Many challenges are red herrings. These are demands that your opponents answer points which in fact are trivial. It can be worth spending thirty seconds trailing a red herring, if your opponents will waste two minutes answering it.

Some Common Errors
Of Tactics

Unwise diversionary skirmishes. Opening on the motion *That the*

Present Level of Unemployment is Unacceptable, a speaker toys with the idea that the level is unacceptably *low,* then cheerfully switches his line and announces that his team will be sporting – they will say unemployment is unacceptably *high.* What did he imagine he was achieving with this diversionary skirmish? Perhaps he felt he was giving a light touch to his opening, or that he might unnerve his opponents. In fact he was both wasting time and (worse) opening his bosom to his adversaries' knife: inviting them to show he was neither serious nor singleminded in his approach to the topic.

Proving more than necessary. On the same motion, I once listened in amazement as the Affirmative leader announced: 'We will prove not only that the present level of unemployment is unacceptable but that *any* level of unemployment is unacceptable.' Why did he do it? Why try to prove two things when the motion required him to prove only one? In the event he made only the lamest attempt to prove the unnecessary, and his opponents harried him unmercifully for his failure.

Complimenting your opponents. Even though you give it an edge of sarcasm, ridicule or irony, a compliment to your opponents is dangerous. 'The Affirmative have thrown down a formidable gauntlet. But we will pick it up, never fear . . .' What a defensive, quaking way to begin your speech – and for no reason.

Agreeing with your adversaries. If at all possible, never agree, admit or concede. Often a Negative leader will say: 'We agree with the Affirmative's definition.' Don't! First because you make it seem (wrongly) as if they have scored off you, and second because as the debate progresses one of your colleagues may want to disagree with part of their definition!

Rhetorical questions. Never ask rhetorical questions ('Does anyone here really *like* income tax?') You will always get the answer you don't want. On one occasion a very experienced speaker asked no fewer than eleven rhetorical questions in succession. The audience responded to every one of them – each time with an answer he did not want. Thereafter he was famous, for having invented a new method of debating: the question–and–answer method, in which the speaker asks the questions and the audience supplies the answers!

Withholding vital information. Some debating teams commonly withhold essential pieces of evidence or argument until their final speaker – in the hope their opponents will not see the strength of their case until it is too late. This ploy is very risky. It can make you seem evasive, and can so weaken the early part of your case that the device becomes self-defeating. Use your best material and argument early, and keep hammering it home by restatement. Above all, never keep back part of your definition – since definition outlines the battleground, the Affirmative's definition and any quarrel the Negative has with it, must come out early. Often withholding of essential information results from possessiveness: the speaker whose research disclosed a juicy piece of evidence wants to use it himself. Wrong. A debate is a team effort. All material should be pooled and shared among the speakers where it will do most good.

What Sort Of Preparation Should You Do?

Whether novices or experts, remind yourselves at the outset of your purpose: to get a clear, reasonable definition; to marshal the strongest arguments for your side; to produce solid well-verified evidence to support those arguments; to argue a balanced, well-knit case through all three speakers; to be constantly aware of the development of your opponents' case: to rebut the main arguments and main evidence they put forward; and (for your leader) to summarise tightly at the end how your opponents' case failed and how yours succeeded.

You will remind yourselves to avoid giving prepared speeches (except for first Affirmative) that ignore what has been said by your opponents; to avoid assertion, which is argument unsupported by evidence; to avoid irrelevance, which is evidence that has not been linked by argument into the proving or disproving of the motion; to avoid mere disagreement with your opponents in the belief that it is rebuttal.

As a rule, it is wise for the whole debating team to meet three times. On the first occasion you will work out the meaning (or alternative meanings) of the motion and what sort of case your team will present. It is essential to do this at the first meeting. Far better to adopt a less than perfect line of argument early in the piece – and leave time to research and hone that line thoroughly – than to choose a quintessential line far too late and fail to research it properly.

The next two meetings are then devoted to preparation. You must work together on this. One way to foster unified thinking is to put the skeleton of your case on a blackboard; or better still on large sheets of paper which can be pinned to the wall, then taken down and put up at the next meeting. The same words are then before you all; if you each take your own notes of discussions you will inevitably record different things, and more easily end up at cross purposes.

The skeleton arguments can be transferred by each speaker onto the 'trigger cards' he will use during the debate. These are the small cards (about 13 cm × 8 cm) on which you will summarise your case and your prepared rebuttal of arguments and evidence that may be used by your opponents. Never write out your speech – just words and phrases, in careful sequence, following the structure of your arguments. With a little practice you will find these trigger words are all you need – moreover they will prevent you giving a 'set speech' and allow you to adapt what you say to what has been said by your opponents.

Simplify! Get rid of big words and technical terms. Paint word pictures. Be systematic. Use pausation to allow your ideas time to sink in with the audience. Above all, don't cram. Be selective. Try to cover no more than four or five main points in your speech. Then tease them out, clarify them. Far better to lodge five points solidly with your listeners than to bewilder them with ten. Remember not only that you must make your meaning clear: you must also take time to show the significance of what you are saying.

Discipline yourself. Fix a mental picture of your allowance of ten minutes. How much of that time will you give to rebuttal, and how much to your own material?

As with your own material, so too with rebuttal. Don't try to rebut everything. Be selective. Ignore red herrings and weak attacks by your opponents. Counter-rebut those attacks that cannot be ignored.

What Should An Adjudicator Look For?

No subject creates so much discussion among debaters as standards of adjudication. As a rule, the best judges are current debaters or those recently retired from debating. Indeed, all debaters should try adjudication, for the two disciplines are interrelated.

A competition debate is unlike a real-life quarrel; it is a display of debating skills by teams who may not personally support the side of the issue that has been allocated to them. To an extent, therefore, it is an artificial exercise. But, for debator and adjudicator alike, it is a salutary discipline to set aside preconceptions and listen as dispassionately as possible to the competing points of view.

Quite the worst crime of an adjudicator is to insert his own views into the debate, judging statements to be right or wrong according to his own opinions. He then becomes, effectively, a participant in the debate; which means the losing team no longer is the one that was beaten by its opponents – but the one that was unfortunate enough to present views the judge did not share! Whenever tempted to say 'I disagreed with . . .' he should ask himself: did the *other* team disagree with that point? If not, it stands.

But what if one team makes a statement the adjudicator knows is wrong yet the other team makes no objection? It stands. First, because it is a matter of chance whether a particular adjudicator will know a piece of evidence is wrong. But more than that: an adjudicator may know a statement made by the Affirmative is wrong, and deduct marks for it; but not know a statement by the Negative is wrong, and fail to deduct marks for it. Manifestly, that is unfair. In other words, the adjudicator must deduct marks for every incorrect statement (and no adjudicator has sufficient knowledge to do that) or for none.

Second, judges often are quite wrong in thinking a piece of evidence is incorrect. It is dangerous to disagree with a speaker who is fresh from researching the subject, on the basis of your remembrance of the facts. Sometimes your 'knowledge' of the inaccuracy may indeed be sound, but often it is not.

Third, the judge who decides a piece of evidence is wrong is, effectively, *rebutting the speaker's evidence without giving him the opportunity of counter-rebuttal*. This, finally, is what is so unfair about adjudicators entering the fray: the job of the debaters is to debate each other, but when the adjudicator inserts his own views into the debate they are hamstrung and cannot respond.

In my opinion, the most searching test of a good judge is whether he can, *with an easy mind,* give marks to a debater for evidence and argument he is convinced are wrong; then wait patiently to see whether an opponent demonstrates they are wrong, in which case he will give good marks to the opponent.

Does all this mean the adjudicator must never use his judgement?

Of course not. His first task is to set aside his biases, prejudices and personal opinions. Then he must use his judgement to decide whether the blows delivered by one team are more telling than the ones received. It is not merely a matter of counting the number of 'hits' each team scores: what matters is how many of the statements are solid punches and how many are light taps.

A skilled adjudicator will ask himself how strong is an item of evidence and how well has it been knitted into the team's case. Is a piece of rebuttal merely chasing an inconsequential red herring; or does it do serious damage to the main thrust of the opposing team's case? Is a particular argument weak or flippant or even loony; or does it come across as persuasive and well-constructed reasoning?

When a speaker uses weak material he must expect it to score low marks; but also he runs the risk that he will present an opportunity to his opponents to score heavily in rebuttal.

What Makes A
Winning Team?

The winning team is not the team that is 'right'. It is the team that out-debates the other. Sometimes a team with indisputably the better side of the issue will lose through missing their opportunities. Thus a deeply religious audience may be in no doubt the Affirmative has won on the motion *That There Is No God* – though none of them supports that side of the issue.

Nor is the winning team necessarily the one that convinces the adjudicator; or that provokes an enthusiastic response from the audience. This is because adjudicators must be able to give decisions against their convictions; and because often audiences are biased.

So the role of the debate adjudicator is: *to listen to what is said between the two teams, ignoring all else including his own opinions on the subject; and to say which team has out-debated the other.*

Of course your task is easy when one team is clearly dominant. Points to watch for:
– Is one team rather scrappy in its case; the other more coherent?
– Is one team on the defensive; the other making all the running?
– Is one team busy patching up its case; the other in control, having anticipated the arguments of its opponents and rebutted them well?
– Is one team oblivious to the ground being made by the other?
– Is one team clearly in flight from the start, 'twisting' the motion

and evading the issue?

How To Assess
Each Speaker

In Chapter 6 we have looked at skills of presentation. As an adjudicator you should score this aspect of each speaker carefully. Overall, you are looking for a persuasive presentation, with an air of conviction and sincerity. The speaker should have presence: he should be in full control of the situation, using voice, pausation, eye contact with the audience, gesture and stance to good persuasive effect. He should be in command, without going too far – a hectoring, declamatory, over-emphatic debater deserves to be marked down.

In assessing content, you should look for the following. Each speaker should demonstrate clear understanding of his team's definition of the motion and main line of argument. His own evidence should be well supported with authorities, should be convincing and tightly knitted into his team's case. He should use argument persuasively to show how his material fits into the structure of his team's case, and advances it. If he descends to assertion, or presents material irrelevantly, he should be penalised. Except for the first Affirmative, all speakers must rebut their opponents vigorously and effectively. Anyone weak on rebuttal must be marked down, for rebuttal is the essence of debating.

Since he opens the show, the leader of the Affirmative gives a prepared speech with no opportunity for rebuttal. You will expect an arresting opening that sets the theme of his team's case: 'Mr Chairman, ladies and gentlemen. There is an old saying that doctors bury their mistakes. If mercy killing is legalised, you can be sure there will be many more buried mistakes . . .' Very quickly, he should go into a clear well-supported definition of the motion, using a good dictionary or other authority for the meaning of any word over which there could be the slightest doubt. You will then expect him to give a clear 'split' of his team's case, outlining the general role of each member of his team including himself, and forecasting the structure of the Affirmative's case. Then you will expect him to give half or more of his time to that part of the case he said he would deal with himself. Finally he should end with a rousing conclusion, dramatically emphasising or summarising his main points. To score well, the leader of the Affirmative must set the scene, grip the

181

imagination of his listeners, and reveal a plausible and convincing framework of his team's case.

Next, the leader of the Negative. He must come out fighting. Attack, attack, attack is the requirement laid upon him. If he does not immediately demonstrate he has a grasp of the entrails of the Affirmative's case he should not score well. If he comes out with what is clearly a prepared opening, ignoring what has been set down by the Affirmative leader, he should be dealt with severely. In particular, if his team is to dispute the meaning of the motion, that should be part of his initial onslaught. Having spent some time (say two or three minutes) on his opening assault, he should then set out clearly the 'split' of his team's case. (Failure of either leader to set out the split, or to do it effectively, should be penalised.) Then the rest of his time (maybe half) will be spent on that portion of his team's case he said he would cover. Ideally, he should weave further rebuttal of the Affirmative leader's material into his own part of the case.

Then comes the second speaker of the Affirmative. In some ways he is the most important of the speakers. Since the Affirmative leader, through coming first in the debate, cannot rebut, then the Affirmative has only two rebuttal speeches. The Negative has three. So if the second Affirmative fails to rebut, or does so briefly or weakly, his team is likely to be in trouble, since that leaves only their third speaker to rebut the Negative's case. And because rebuttal (attacking the other team's case) is the essence of debating, three strong rebuttal speeches on the Negative will probably defeat only one on the Affirmative. Thus the second Affirmative must come out attacking and spend two or three or four minutes in rebuttal and counter-rebuttal. To a degree, his role is the same as first Negative: he is the first member of his team who can attack their opponents' case, and he must not fail to strike. Many second Affirmative speakers do not appreciate their attacking role, and give a prepared speech. An adjudicator must penalise any failure of second Affirmative to attack the first Negative or to shore up the attack made on his own leader's case. The rest of the second Affirmative's speech should be solid evidence and argument: the backbone of his team's case. He must of course cover what his leader said he would and ideally should use his own material as further rebuttal where he can.

The second Negative, too, must attack – particularly the arguments of the second Affirmative but also of the Affirmative leader. Then he should devote about six minutes to the backbone of his team's case. He too must cover that part of the case his leader said he would, and should try to use his own case as either direct or parallel rebuttal.

Both third speakers have similar tasks: to spend about half their time rebutting the opponents who have preceded them, and in patching up whatever serious holes have been opened up in the evidence and argument of their own preceding speakers. Finally, each will spend about five minutes covering that part of his team's case allocated to him by his leader.

Throughout, the judge must assess the quality of evidence and argument, be watchful for irrelevance and assertion, and mark accordingly.

In the leaders' summaries the adjudicator will expect to see good allocation of time. First, a statement of the main points of the opponents' case and where it was wrong (maybe two and a half minutes); then finishing with the main points of his own team's case, why it is the right one and how it survived attack (maybe three minutes), then perhaps a dramatic thirty-second concluding burst. A common failing is to spend too much time on the other team's case, neglecting to do justice to one's own; such failure must be severely penalised for the summaries should tie together the main elements of the debate. The most skilful summarisers are able to weave together the strands of both cases, revealing the cut and counter-cut (of course, to their own team's advantage) that occurred as the debate was played out. The adjudicator will look for an understanding of the main arguments that were at issue; and will penalise a scrappy, episodic summary that wastes time on points of detail.

In particular, the judge will score heavily the leader who demonstrates inconsistencies, disagreements and internal muddlement in the opposing team's case. To show that the members of the other team have inadvertently quarrelled with each other is devastating in a summary.

Teamwork And Generalship

Whether these elements are marked separately (as some marksheets provide) or are included in the overall marks for each speaker, they are important. Since a debate is a team event each speaker must link with his colleagues, support them by counter-rebutting the attacks made upon them, and tie his own evidence and argument into the establishment of the team case. That's teamwork. Generalship is somewhat different. It is the capacity of a speaker to 'read' the progress of the dispute; to see the main lines of argument of each side and how they are interacting; to recognise dangerous forays by his opponents and deal effectively with them; to massage and mould the shape of the developing contest in the way he presents his own evidence, argument and rebuttal. Good generalship is very persuasive and deserves high marks.

A poor general will waste time chasing trivia; will be diverted by the red herrings trailed by his opponents; will use his time badly and often find it has run out before he has delivered his part of his team's case; and will fail to see the other team making ground. He must be marked accordingly.

Note that the Affirmative leader displays generalship by the way he sets out his team's case, shutting out opportunities that otherwise would have been open to the Negative, and generally directing the dispute the way he wants it to go.

How Should You
Allocate Marks?

An adjudicator must carry through his open-mindedness to the end. He should beware of trying to identify a 'knockout blow', scored by one speaker, which in his view will render the rest of the debate futile. It is extremely dangerous for any judge to say, 'I put down my pen after the first Negative had spoken, for he had destroyed the Affirmative's case.'

Some adjudicators search constantly for knockout blows: 'When the second Affirmative brought out that piece of evidence, he convinced me of his team's case . . .' Here the judge is both searching for a knockout blow *and* inserting his own views into the debate.

There is much dispute among adjudicators about the correct method of scoring a debate where one team is very funny, but weak in argument; while the other team is plodding in its presentation but strong in argument. Should the judge favour the team with the sparkling presentation; or the one with solid argument?

This dilemma greatly bothers many adjudicators; but should not. I suggest the correct method is to score the bright team high for presentation and low for material; score the dull team low for presentation and high for material; then see which team has the higher combined mark. It is simply a question of whose is the greater superiority: does the superiority of team A in presentation outweigh the superiority of team B in material?

How, then, do you allocate your marks? If you are bound by a particular marksheet, that's that. If not, I suggest each of the main speakers be marked out of 100, as follows:

– 40 marks for presentation (chiefly use of voice, pausation, stance, gesture, eye contact with audience, humour).
– 40 marks for material (chiefly evidence, argument, rebuttal).
– 20 marks for generalship (chiefly structure, teamwork, persuasiveness, reading of the cut and thrust of the main arguments of each side).

Each leader's summary will additionally be marked out of 50, concentrating in particular on the way he draws together the main strands of the debate, but again giving marks for presentation, material and generalship.

Every adjudicator must decide: 'What shall be my spread of marks?' Timid adjudicators compress their marks. If each main speech carries a maximum of 100, a timorous judge may allocate the speakers between 70 and 78 marks. Rarely are six speakers so closely matched. You should not be afraid to give (say) 45 marks to one speaker who performs badly, while giving between 60 and 85 marks to the remainder. Almost certainly that bad speaker (who perhaps spoke so quickly he was seldom comprehensible) will lose the debate for his side; whereas if you compress the marks, his side may, in the evening out of things, scrape to victory.

Some adjudicators take no notes. They like to let the debate 'wash over me' and come to a decision at the end as to 'which team convinced me'. This is dangerous, and risks the insertion of the adjudicator's own views into the debate. Also, if the argument has been closely fought, he will have difficulty comparing the later speakers with the earlier ones. And failure to take notes can thwart his attempt to give guidance to the speakers when presenting his adjudication.

How many judges should there be? For any important event, especially the final of a major competition, there should be three. Adjudication is so subjective that it is unwise to rely on one judge if it can be avoided. Should the adjudicators confer? Preferably not .

Ideally, I believe, the adjudicators should be experienced debaters – preferably still competing. Wherever possible both teams should be invited to agree upon the judge or judges. Much politicking and manoeuvring goes on in the choice of adjudicators, but I believe no team should have to be judged by someone in whom they have no faith. Only where no agreement can be reached between the teams should the organisers impose an adjudicator.

Adjudication of competition debates is not an academic exercise. Its benefits for real-life situations should be obvious. You become a trained analyst, able to distinguish assertion from evidence, humbug from sincerity, dishonest argument from rigorous logic, mere disputatiousness from effective rebuttal.

Above all, you learn that in many of the contentious issues that divide people there is no absolute right or wrong. As evidence and argument accumulate, so the balance of your judgement may tend to tip one way or the other. And even when all the evidence of one dispute is in, and your judgement is formed, that is not necessarily an end of the matter. For tomorrow the dispute may re-open, more evidence and argument may be presented, and if you remain open-minded you may find yourself reversing your judgement of today!

Summary

1. Good generalship can outwit an opponent who has superior material.

2. Turning your opponents' evidence to your advantage can destroy them.

3. Knowing how to exert pressure on your opponents (and resist their pressure) can give you winning momentum.

4. Avoid the common errors of tactics that open your case to unnecessary threat.

5. The skills of debate and adjudication are inter-related.

6. The worst crime of an adjudicator is to insert his own views into the debate.

7. Judges must be able to separate assertion from rebuttal, be watchful for irrelevancy, and decide which team has out-debated the other.

Epilogue

GO OUT THERE AND
HAVE A BALL

You are in a large hall, one of an audience of a hundred people. Up on stage the master of ceremonies clutches the microphone and says: 'At this point, ladies and gentlemen, I must stop. There is someone in the audience whose views we really must have. So I call to the microphone . . .' Here he pauses, looks directly at you, and mentions your name.

What should you do? Crawl under the seat? Rush headlong from the building? Fake a heart attack?

Stand slowly. Start thinking immediately of what you will say when you reach the microphone. Keep ordering your thoughts as you shuffle sideways to the aisle. Continue to ruminate as you walk unhurriedly to the platform and mount the steps. *That's the secret*: don't become self-conscious. Don't get flustered and begin worrying that you are the centre of attention. Concentrate. Forget the audience. Grasp quickly what will be your theme; your opening words; your conclusion. You have no time to be distracted by thoughts of the audience.

An impromptu speech is always a severe test. Many competent people dodge such opportunities with the inward wail: how can I be expected to speak entirely without preparation?

In a sense, you cannot. There is no such thing as a truly impromptu speech. You are the sum of your past experiences and knowledge; your impromptu speeches are drawn from that well of information, ideas, opinions, attitudes; and so to a degree are your prepared speeches. Of course, the better informed you are on a wide range of issues, the deeper will be the well from which you draw your impromptu statements. And the more you learn about the world, the more you practise developing lines of argument, the better will be your off-the-cuff utterances.

Remember these techniques: when asked to give your views at

short notice, pause, reflect. What will be your theme and your conclusion? How will you start so that you can develop your theme and work up to your conclusion?

The best impromptu speeches are as good as the best prepared speeches; they grow out of the beliefs and past thinking of inquiring, knowledge-seeking people who are used to isolating the heart of an issue and taking a stand on it. When combined with speaking skills and techniques, your store of knowledge will produce memorable communications. Indeed, the accumulated memories and ideas of your lifetime are your most important aid in the speeches you give, at work and at play.

In this book we have talked about ways of overcoming the platform nervousness to which everyone is prone. We have discussed the art of lively presentation; looked at the uses of humour and how to make it work for you; and discovered how to win over a hostile audience. We have examined speech structures and methods of research; how to use words effectively and vividly; and we have seen how the skills of debate can be of value in your everyday utterances. We have learned much about the fine arts of social speaking, of chairmanship, of job interviews, and of dealing with the news media.

All of these speaking skills are interrelated. Each reinforces and supports the other. It is not true that public speaking is 'just conversation turned up loud'. When speaking in public you are on your own and must get it right first time – and what is right depends very much on the occasion.

But finally I must say this. You cannot learn skydiving from a book: sooner or later you must take a header from the aeroplane. So too with public speaking. Grab every invitation. You must hurl yourself from aeroplanes as often as you can. I hope the pages of this book will provide a safe parachute. Do remember to enjoy the scenery on the way down.

And many happy landings.